PETER WEISS'

The Persecution and Assassination of Jean-Paul Marat As Performed by the Inmates of the Asylum of Charenton Under the Direction of the Marquis De Sade

English version by
GEOFFREY SKELTON

Verse adaptation by
ADRIAN MITCHELL

an attack on # the Enlightenment and the French Revolution

Dramatic Publishing
Woodstock, Illinois • London, England • Melbourne, Australia

*** NOTICE ***

THE PERSECUTION AND ASSASSINATION OF
JEAN PAUL MARAT AS PERFORMED BY THE INMATES OF
THE ASYLUM OF CHARENTON UNDER THE DIRECTION OF
THE MARQUIS DE SADE
Published originally under the title of "Die Verfolgung und Ermordung
Jean Paul Marats dargestellt durch die Schauspielgruppe des Hospizes
zu Charenton unter Anleitung des Herrn de Sade."

The Music composed by Richard Peaslee used in the original Broadway production of the Play, is available for use in stock and amateur productions. To obtain piano and vocal scores and Music rental rates contact E.C. Shermer, 138 Ipswich Street, Boston, MA 02215.

For Play royalty rates contact Dramatic Publishing.

THE PERSECUTION AND ASSASSINATION OF JEAN-PAUL MARAT AS PERFORMED BY THE INMATES OF THE ASYLUM OF CHARENTON UNDER THE DIRECTION OF THE MARQUIS DE SADE

A Play in Two Acts

For Nine Men, Three Women, Bit Parts and Others

[CHARACTERS]

MARQUIS DE SADE
COULMIER
JEAN-PAUL MARAT
SIMONNE EVRARD
CHARLOTTE CORDAY
DUPERRET
JACQUES ROUX
HERALD
CUCURUCU
POLPOCH
KOKOL
ROSSIGNOL

[BIT PARTS]

MOTHER
FATHER
SCHOOLMASTER
MILITARY REPRESENTATIVE
SCIENTIST
NEWLY RICH
VOLTAIRE
LAVOISIER
SEVERAL PATIENTS

4

[NON-SPEAKING PARTS]

COULMIER'S WIFE and DAUGHTER
MALE NURSES
PATIENTS
SISTERS
MUSICIANS
CHORUS

PLACE: *The asylum of Charenton.*

TIME: *1808.*

ACT ONE

The asylum bell rings behind the stage. The curtain rises.

1. ASSEMBLY

The stage shows the bath hall of the asylum. To right and left bathtubs and showers. Against the back wall a many-tiered platform with benches and massage tables. In the middle area of the stage benches are placed for the actors, sisters and male nurses. The walls are covered with white tiles to a height of about ten feet. There are window openings high up in the side walls. There is a metal framework in front of the platform and around the baths at the sides. Curtains are fixed to each side of the framework before the platform and these can be pulled when the patients are to be hidden. Front stage centre there is a circular arena. To the right of it a dais for Marat's bath, to the left a dais for Sade's chair. Left front a raised tribunal for Coulmier and his family. On another tribunal right front the musicians stand ready.

SADE is occupied with last-minute preparations for the entry of the actors. The MALE NURSES are completing a few routine operations of bathing and massage. Patients are sitting or lying on the platform at the back. SADE gives a sign. Through a side door at right back the actors enter, led by COULMIER and his family and escorted by SISTERS

and MALE NURSES. The PATIENTS rise to their
feet. The ceremonious procession comes forward.
The asylum bell is still tolling. MARAT, wrapped
in a white sheet and accompanied by SIMONNE, is
led to the bath.   CORDAY, sunk into herself, is
taken to a bench by two sisters. DUPERRET, ROUX
and the FOUR SINGERS take up their positions as
COULMIER reaches the stage. The HERALD stands
in the middle of the stage.   SADE stands near his
raised chair.   The tolling of the bell ceases. The
procession moves toward the acting area. COUL-
MIER enters the acting area.   The PATIENTS in
the background stand tensely.   One of them adopts
an eccentric pose, another comes slowly forward
with outstretched arms.

FANFARE.

2. PROLOGUE

COULMIER
As Director of the Clinic of Charenton
I would like to welcome you to this salon
To one of our residents a vote
of thanks is due Monsieur de Sade who wrote
and has produced this play for your delectation
and for our patients' rehabilitation
We ask your kindly indulgence for
a cast never on stage before
coming to Charenton But each inmate
I can assure you will try to pull his weight
We're modern enlightened and we don't agree
with locking up patients We prefer therapy
through education and especially art
so that our hospital may play its part
faithfully following according to our lights
the Declaration of Human Rights
I agree with our author Monsieur de Sade

that his play set in our modern bath house won't be
    marred
by all these instruments for mental and physical
    hygiene
Quite on the contrary they set the scene
For in Monsieur de Sade's play he has tried
to show how Jean-Paul Marat died
and how he waited in his bath before
Charlotte Corday came knocking at his door

3. PREPARATION

HERALD knocks three times with his staff and gives
the orchestra a sign. Ceremonious music begins.
COULMIER moves to his family. SADE mounts his
dais. MARAT is placed in his bath. SIMONNE puts
his bandage straight. The SISTERS arrange Corday's
costume. The group assumes the pose of a heroic
tableau.

4. PRESENTATION

The music stops.

                (HERALD knocks three times with his
                staff.)

                HERALD
Already seated in his place
here is Marat observe his face
                (Points his staff at MARAT.)
Fifty years old and not yet dead
he wears a bandage around his head
                (Points staff at bandage.)
His flesh burns it is yellow as cheese
                (Points at his neck.)
because disfigured by a skin disease

And only water cooling every limb
        (Points to bath.)
prevents his fever from consuming him
          (MARAT takes his pen and begins to
          write.)
To act this most important role we chose
a lucky paranoic one of those
who've made unprecedented strides since we
introduced them to hydrotherapy
The lady who is acting as his nurse
          (Points at SIMONNE. She bends with a
          jerky movement over MARAT, loosens
          his bandage and puts on a new one.)
whose touch certainly makes him no worse
is Simonne Evrard not Charlotte Corday
Marat and Evrard united one day
They shared one vision of the just and true
and furthermore they shared her money too
Here's Charlotte Corday waiting for her entry
          (Points to CORDAY who smoothes her
          clothes and ties her neckcloth.)
She comes from Caen her family landed gentry
Her dress is pretty shoes chic and you'll note
She readjusts the cloth around her throat
          (Points at it. CORDAY adjusts it.)
Historians agree so it's not lewd in us
to say that she's phenomenally pulchritudinous
          (She draws herself up.)
Unfortunately the girl who plays the role here
has sleeping sickness also melancholia
Our hope must be for this afflicted soul
          (With closed eyes, she inclines her head
          far backwards.)
that she does not forget her role
          (With emphasis, turning to CORDAY.)
Ah here comes Monsieur Duperret
          (Indicates DUPERRET.)

with silken hose and fresh toupee
To the Revolution's murderous insanity
he brings a touch of high urbanity
Though as a well-known Girondist
his name's upon Marat's black list
he's handsome cheerful full of zest
and needs more watching than the rest

> (DUPERRET approaches CORDAY, paw-
> ing her furtively. The HERALD raps him
> on the hand with his staff. A SISTER pulls
> back DUPERRET.)

Jailed for taking a radical view
of anything you can name the former priest Jacques
        Roux

> (Indicates ROUX who pushes out his el-
> bows and raises his head.)

Ally of Marat's revolution but
unfortunately the censor's cut
most of his rabble-rousing theme
Our moral guardians found it too extreme

ROUX

Liberty

> (Opens his mouth and pushes his elbows
> out vigorously. COULMIER raises his
> forefinger threateningly.)

HERALD

Ladies and gentlemen our players
are drawn from many social layers

> (He waves his staff over the audience
> and the group of actors.)

Our singers for example of these four
each must be classified as bottom drawer
But now they've left the alcoholic mists
of slums and gin cellars our vocalists

> (Points to the FOUR SINGERS.)

Cucurucu Polpoch Kokol
and on the streets no longer Rossignol
   (Each named changes his pose with a
   studied bow, ROSSIGNOL curtsies.)
Now meet this gentleman from high society
   (Points at SADE who turns his back on
   the public in a bored way.)
who under the lurid star of notoriety
came to live with us just five years ago
It's to his genius that we owe this show
The former Marquis Monsieur de Sade
whose books were banned his essays barred
while he's been persecuted and reviled
thrown into jail and for some years exiled
The introduction's over now the play
of Jean-Paul Marat can get under way
Tonight the date
is the thirteenth of July eighteen-o-eight
And on this night our cast intend
showing how fifteen years ago night without end
fell on that man that invalid
   (Points at MARAT.)
And you are going to see him bleed
   (Points at Marat's breast.)
and see this woman after careful thought
   (Points at CORDAY.)
take up the dagger and cut him short

[Homage to Marat]

   (Music starts. CORDAY is led by the
   SISTERS from the arena to a bench in
   the background. SIMONNE seats herself on the edge of the dais behind Marat's
   bath. SADE goes to his seat and sits
   down. ROUX and DUPERRET withdraw
   to a bench. The FOUR SINGERS take

their position for the homage to MARAT.)

5. HOMAGE TO MARAT

KOKOL and POLPOCH
(Recitative.)
Four years after the Revolution
and the old king's execution
four years after remember how
those courtiers took their final bow

CHORUS
(Singing in the background.)
String up every aristocrat
Out with the priests and let them live on their fat

CUCURUCU and ROSSIGNOL
(Recitative.)
Four years after we started fighting
Marat keeps on with his writing
Four years after the Bastille fell
he still recalls the old battle yell

CHORUS
(Singing in the background.)
Down with all of the ruling class
Throw all the generals out on their arse

ROUX
Long live the Revolution
(The FOUR SINGERS and other PATIENTS
form an adoring group around the bath. A
wreath of leaves is held up.)

PATIENT
(In background.)
Marat we won't dig our own bloody graves

PATIENT
(In background.)
Marat we've got to be clothed a .d fed

PATIENT
(In background.)
Marat we're sick of working like slaves

PATIENT
(In background.)
Marat we've got to have cheaper bread

KOKOL
(Indicating wreath.)
We crown you with these leaves Marat
.because of the laurel shortage
The laurels all went to decorate
academics generals and heads of state
And their heads are enormous
(The wreath is placed on Marat's head,
he is lifted from the bath and carried
on the shoulders of two PATIENTS.)

CHORUS
Good old Marat
By your side we'll stand or fall
You're the only one that we can trust at all
(MARAT is carried around the arena.
SIMONNE walks beside him looking up
to him anxiously. The FOUR SINGERS
and the PATIENTS in the procession
carry out studied gestures of homage.)

ROSSIGNOL
(Naively, taking the play seriously.)
Don't scratch your scabs or they'll never get any
better

FOUR SINGERS

Four years he fought and he fought unafraid
sniffing down traitors by traitors betrayed
Marat in the courtroom Marat underground
sometimes the otter and sometimes the hound

Fighting all the gentry and fighting every priest
businessman the bourgeois the military beast
Marat always ready to stifle every scheme
of the sons of the arse-licking dying regime

We've got new generals our leaders are new
They sit and they argue and all that they do
is sell their own colleagues and ride on their backs
and jail them and break them or give them all the
    axe

Screaming in language no man understands
of rights that we grabbed with our own bleeding
    hands
when we wiped out the bosses and stormed through
    the wall
of the prison they told us would outlast us all

/Marat We're Poor/

CHORUS and FOUR SINGERS

Marat we're poor and the poor stay poor
Marat don't make us wait any more
We want our rights and we don't care how
We want our revolution *now*.

            (MARAT is ceremoniously placed back
            in the bath.   The wreath is taken from
            his head.   SIMONNE busily changes his
            bandages and rearranges the cloth about
            his shoulders.   Music ends.   SADE sits
            unmoving, looking across the stage with

a mocking expression on his face.)

HERALD
The Revolution came and went
and unrest was replaced by discontent

6. STIFLED UNREST

PATIENT
We've got rights the right to starve

PATIENT
We've got jobs waiting for work

PATIENT
We're all brothers lousy and dirty

PATIENT
We're all free and equal to die like dogs

ROSSIGNOL
And now our lovely new leaders come
they give us banknotes which we're told
are money just as good as gold
but they're only good for wiping your bum
            (COULMIER jumps up from his seat.)

ROUX
            (In the middle of the stage.)
Who controls the markets
Who locks up the granaries
Who got the loot from the palaces
Who sits tight on the estates
that were going to be divided between the poor
            (COULMIER looks around. A SISTER
            pulls ROUX back.)

PATIENTS
(In the background, and beating out the
rhythm emphatically.)
Who keeps up prisoner
Who locks us in
We're all normal and we want our freedom

CHORUS
Freedom Freedom Freedom
(The unrest grows.)

COULMIER
(Knocking with his stick on the railing.)
Monsieur de Sade
(SADE takes no notice.)
It appears I must act as the voice of reason
What's going to happen when right at the start of
     the play
the patients are so disturbed
Please keep your production under control
Times have changed times are different
and these days we should take a subtler view
of old grievances
(The PATIENTS are pushed back by the
MALE NURSES. Some SISTERS place
themselves in front of the PATIENTS and
sing a tranquilizing litany. Midstage,
CORDAY, who is sitting slumped down
on the bench, is being prepared by the
SISTERS for her entrance.)

HERALD
Here sits Marat the people's choice
dreaming and listening to his fever's voice
You see his hand curled round his pen
and the screams from the street are all forgotten
He stares at the map of France eyes marching from

town to town
>(Points to the map, which MARAT rolls up.)

while you wait
>(Turns around. In the background a whispering begins and spreads.)

CHORUS
(Whispers.)

Corday Corday

HERALD
While you wait for this woman to cut him down
>(Points with his staff to CORDAY. Orchestra plays the Corday theme. Waiting for the SISTERS to complete their preparation.)

And none of us

And none of us
>(CORDAY is led forward by the SISTERS.)

And none of us can alter the fact do what we will

that she stands outside his door ready and poised
>to kill
>(He taps the floor three times with his staff. CORDAY is put in position in the arena. This all resembles a ritual act. The music ends. The SISTERS step back.)

CORDAY
(Sleepily and hesitantly.)

Poor Marat in your bathtub

your body soaked saturated with poison
>(Waking up.)

Poison spurting from your hiding place

poisoning the people

arousing them to looting and murder

Marat

I have come

I
Charlotte Corday from Caen
where a huge army of liberation is massing
and Marat I come as the first of them Marat
             (Pause. A chord on the lute leads in the
             musical accompaniment.)

             [Corday Waltz]

Once both of us saw the world must go
and change as we read in great Rousseau
but change meant one thing to you I see
and something quite different to me
The very same words we both have said
to give our ideals wings to spread
     but my way was true
     while for you
the highway led over mountains of dead

Once both of us spoke a single tongue
of brotherly love we sweetly sung
but love meant one thing to you I see
and something quite different to me
but now I'm aware that I was blind
and now I can see into your mind
     and so I say no
     and I go
to murder you Marat and free all mankind
             (Music ends.   CORDAY stands with her
             head bowed. The SISTERS lead her back.)

8. I AM THE REVOLUTION

                    MARAT
             (Tyrannically.)
Simonne Simonne
More cold water

Change my bandage
O this itching is unbearable
> (SIMONNE stands ready behind him and
> carries out with maniacal movements her
> rehearsed tasks. She changes his band-
> age, fans him with the shoulder cloth and
> tips a jug over the bath.)

SIMONNE

Jean-Paul don't scratch yourself
you'll tear your skin to shreds
give up writing Jean-Paul
it won't do any good

MARAT

My call
My fourteenth of July call
to the people of France

SIMONNE

Jean-Paul please be more careful
look how red the water's getting

MARAT

And what's a bath full of blood
compared to the bloodbaths still to come
Once we thought a few hundred corpses would be
    enough
then we saw thousands were still too few
and today we can't even count all the dead
Everywhere you look
everywhere
> (MARAT raises himself up in the bath.
> The FOUR SINGERS stretched out on the
> floor play cards, taking no notice of
> MARAT.)

There they are

Behind the walls
Up on the rooftops
Down in the cellars
Hypocrites
They wear the people's cap on their heads
but their underwear's embroidered with crowns
and if so much as a shop gets looted
they squeal
Beggars villains gutter rats
Simonne Simonne
my head's on fire
I can't breathe
There is a rioting mob inside me
Simonne
I am the Revolution
                    (CORDAY is led forward by the SISTERS.)

9. CORDAY'S FIRST VISIT

                    (HERALD taps three times with his staff
                    on the floor and points at CORDAY, who
                    is led on to the arena.   DUPERRET fol-
                    lows CORDAY and remains with bent knee
                    at the edge of the arena. SIMONNE stands
                    between her and the bath.)

                              HERALD
Corday's first visit
                    (Orchestra plays the Corday theme.)

                              CORDAY
I have come to speak to Citizen Marat
I have an important message for him
about the situation in Caen my home
where his enemies are gathering

                              SIMONNE
We don't want any visitors

We want a bit of peace
If you've got anything to say to Marat
put it in writing

CORDAY

What I have to say cannot be said in writing
I want to stand in front of him and look at him
          (Amorously.)
I want to see his body tremble and his forehead
     bubble with sweat
I want to thrust right between his ribs the dagger
which I carry between my breasts
          (Obsessively.)
I shall take the dagger in both hands
and push it through his flesh
and then I will hear
          (Approaches MARAT.)
what he has got to say to me
               (She stands directly in front of the bath.
               She raises dagger and is poised to strike.
               SIMONNE stands paralysed. SADE rises
               from his seat.)

SADE

Not yet Corday
You have to come to his door three times
               (CORDAY stops short, hides the dagger
               and withdraws to her bench. The SISTERS
               and DUPERRET follow her as she leaves.)

10. SONG AND MIME OF CORDAY'S ARRIVAL IN
    PARIS

               (As an accompaniment to the song, PA-
               TIENTS come forward as mimes. They
               walk singly around the arena. With simple
               disguises they present types in the streets.

One is an 'Incroyable' another a 'Merveil-
leuse' or a banner-bearer, a salesman
and cutler, an acrobat or flower seller,
and there are also some prostitutes.
CORDAY circles the arena in the opposite
direction. She represents the country
girl who has come to town for the first
time.)

[Song and Mime of Corday's Arrival in Paris]

FOUR SINGERS
(On the edge of the arena, to a musical
accompaniment. Song.)
Charlotte Corday came to our town
heard the people talking saw the banners wave
Weariness had almost dragged her down
weariness had dragged her down

Charlotte Corday had to be brave
she could never stay at comfortable hotels
Had to find a man with knives to sell
had to find a man with knives

Charlotte Corday passed the pretty stores
Perfume and cosmetics powders and wigs
unguent for curing syphilis sores
unguent for curing your sores

She saw a dagger its handle was white
walked into the cutlery seller's door
When she saw the dagger the dagger was bright
Charlotte saw the dagger was bright

When the man asked her who is it for
it is common knowledge to each of you
Charlotte smiled and paid him his forty sous

Charlotte smiled and paid forty sous
                    (Mime of the purchase of the knife.   COR-
                    DAY chooses the dagger, takes it and
                    pays. She conceals the dagger under her
                    neck-cloth.   The SALESMAN looks down
                    her bosom with an admiring gesture.)
Charlotte Corday walked alone
Paris birds sang sugar calls
Charlotte walked down lanes of stone
through the haze from perfume stalls
Charlotte smelt the dead's gangrene
Heard the singing guillotine
                    (The mime procession grows larger and
                    develops into a dance of death. The music
                    underlines the monotonous rhythm. Two
                    PATIENTS, covered with a cloth, repre-
                    sent a horse. They pull a cart in which
                    stand the condemned receiving last rites
                    from a priest. The PATIENTS accompa-
                    nying the cart make ecstatic and contort-
                    ed movements.   Some are seized with
                    convulsions and throw themselves down
                    in fits.   One hears stifled giggles and
                    groans and the stamping of feet to music.)

                    /The Tumbrel Song/

Don't soil your pretty little shoes
The gutter's deep and red
Climb up climb up and ride along with me
the tumbrel driver said

But she never said a word
never turned her head

Don't soil your pretty little pants
I only go one way

Climb up climb up and ride along with me
There's no gold coach today.

But she never said a word
never turned her head

                    CORDAY
              (In front of the arena, turned to the public.
              Behind her the stamping continues.)
What kind of town is this
The sun can hardly pierce the haze
not a haze made out of rain and fog
but steaming thick and hot
like the mist in a slaughterhouse
Why are they howling
What are they dragging through the streets
They carry stakes but what's impaled on those
      stakes
Why do they hop what are they dancing for
Why are they racked with laughter
Why do the children scream
What are those heaps they fight over
those heaps with eyes and mouths
What kind of town is this
hacked buttocks lying in the street
What are all these faces
              (Behind her the dance of death takes place.
              The FOUR SINGERS join the dancers. The
              cart is turned into a place of execution.
              Two PATIENTS represent the guillotine.
              The execution is prepared in gruesome
              detail.   CORDAY sits slumped at the
              foremost edge of the arena.)
Soon these faces will close around me
These eyes and mouths will call me to join them
              (The mime depicts the piercing and burst-
              ing of the fat belly of the priest. The
              condemned man leans across the execution
              block. His hands are sawn off.)

11. DEATH'S TRIUMPH

MARAT
(Speaking to the audience.)
Now it's happening and you can't stop it happening
The people used to suffer everything
now they take their revenge
You are watching that revenge
and you don't remember that you drove the people
    to it
Now you protest
but it's too late
to start crying over spilt blood
What is the blood of these aristocrats
compared with the blood the people shed for you
Many of them had their throats slit by your gangs
Many of them died more slowly in your workshops

> (The hands of the victim fall off. Howls.
> The executioners start sawing off his
> head.)

So what is this sacrifice
compared with the sacrifices the people made
to keep you fat
What are a few looted mansions
compared with their looted lives
You don't care
if the foreign armies with whom you're making
    secret deals
march in and massacre the people
You hope the people will be wiped out so you can
    flourish
and when they are wiped out not a muscle will
    twitch in your puffy bourgeois faces
which are now all twisted up with anger and disgust

> (COULMIER rises. The head falls off.
> Triumphant screams. The PATIENTS
> play ball with the head.)

COULMIER

Monsieur de Sade
we can't allow this
you really cannot call this education
It isn't making my patients any better
they're all becoming over-excited
After all we invited the public here
to show them that our patients
are not all social lepers

(SADE does not react. He gazes with a
mocking smile across the stage and cues
the HERALD.)

HERALD

(Tapping his staff before COULMIER has
finished speaking.)

We only show these people massacred
because this indisputably occurred
Please calmly watch these barbarous displays
which could not happen nowadays
The men of that time mostly now demised
were primitive we are more civilised

(HERALD points with his staff at the execution scene. Trumpet call. Procession
of nobles forms quickly, lining up for
execution.)

CORDAY

(Rising.)

Up there on the scaffold
you stand completely still and stare
farther than your executioners can see
That is how I will stand
when it's all over

(She closes her eyes and appears to be
sleeping.)

SADE

Look at them Marat
these men who once owned everything
See how they turn their defeat into victory
Now that their pleasures have been taken away
the guillotine saves them from endless boredom
Gaily they offer their heads as if for coronation
Is not that the pinnacle of perversion

> (The victims kneel in front of the execu-
> tion block. SADE gestures to the whole
> group to retreat. The PATIENTS with-
> draw. The cart is taken away. CORDAY
> is led to her bench. A curtain is drawn
> to hide the PATIENTS.)

12. CONVERSATION CONCERNING LIFE AND DEATH

> (Order is restored at the back. The SIS-
> TERS murmur a short litany.)

MARAT

> (Speaking to SADE across the empty arena.)

I read in your books de Sade
in one of your immortal works
that the basis of all of life is death

SADE

Correct Marat
But man has given a false importance to death
Any animal plant or man who dies
adds to Nature's compost heap
becomes the manure without which
nothing could grow nothing could be created
Death is simply part of the process
Every death even the cruellest death
drowns in the total indifference of Nature

compared to ideals of Enlightenment

Nature herself would watch unmoved
if we destroyed the entire human race
            (Rising.)
I hate Nature
this passionless spectator this unbreakable iceberg-
    face
that can bear everything
this goads us to greater and greater acts
            (Breathing heavily.)
Haven't we always beaten down those weaker than
    ourselves
Haven't we torn at their throats
with continuous villainy and lust
Haven't we experimented in our laboratories
before applying the final solution
Let me remind you of the execution of Damiens
after his unsuccessful attempt to assassinate
Louis the Fifteenth (now deceased)
Remember how Damiens died
How gentle the guillotine is
compared with his torture
It lasted four hours while the crowd goggled
and Casanova at an upper window
felt under the skirts of the ladies watching
            (Pointing in the direction of the tribunal
            where COULMIER sits.)
His chest arms thighs and calves were slit open
Molten lead was poured into each slit
boiling oil they poured over him burning tar wax
    sulphur
They burnt off his hands
tied ropes to his arms and legs
harnessed four horses to him and geed them up
They pulled at him for an hour but they'd never
    done it before
and he wouldn't come apart
until they sawed through his shoulders and hips

So he lost the first arm then the second
and he watched what they did to him and then turned
    to us
and shouted so everyone could understand
And when they tore off the first leg and then the
    second leg
he still lived though his voice was getting weak
and at the end he hung there a bloody torso with a
    nodding head
just groaning and staring at the crucifix
which the father confessor was holding up to him
        (In the background a half-murmured
        litany is heard.)
That   *the people*
was a festival with which   *found pleasure in*
today's festivals can't compete *his torture*
Even our inquisition gives us no pleasure
nowadays
Although we've only just started
there's no passion in our post-revolutionary
    murders
Now they are all official
We condemn to death without emotion
and there's no singular personal death to be had
only an anonymous cheapened death
which we could dole out to entire nations
on a mathematical basis
until the time comes
for all life
to be extinguished

MARAT

Citizen Marquis
you may have fought for us last September
when we dragged out of the gaols
the aristocrats who plotted against us
but you still talk like a grand seigneur

and what you call the indifference of Nature
is your own lack of compassion

SADE

Compassion
Now Marat you are talking like an aristocrat
Compassion is the property of the privileged class-
es
When the pitier lowers himself
to give to a beggar
he throbs with contempt
To protect his riches he pretends to be moved
and his gift to the beggar amounts to no more than
a kick (lute chord)
No Marat
no small emotions please
Your feelings were never petty
For you just as for me
only the most extreme actions matter

MARAT

If I am extreme I am not extreme in the same way
as you
Against Nature's silence I use action
In the vast indifference I invent a meaning
I don't watch unmoved I intervene
and say that this and this are wrong
and I work to alter them and improve them
The important thing
is to pull yourself up by your own hair
to turn yourself inside out
and see the whole world with fresh eyes

13. MARAT'S LITURGY

(The curtain is drawn open. PATIENTS
move forward and arrange themselves in

a closed group.)

HERALD
Marat's liturgy

MARAT
Remember how it used to be
The kings were our dear fathers
under whose care we lived in peace
and their deeds were glorified
by official poets
Piously the simpleminded breadwinners
passed on the lesson to their children

CHORUS
(Murmuring in the background as MARAT
continues.)
The kings are our dear fathers
under whose care we live in peace
The kings are our dear fathers
under whose care we live in peace

MARAT
And the children repeated the lesson they believed it
as anyone believes
what they hear over and over again
(CHORUS repeats.)
And over and over again the priests said
(Accompanied by chorus of PATIENTS.)
Our love embraces all mankind
of every colour race and creed
Our love is international universal
we are all brothers every one
(Continuing alone.)
And the priests looked down into the pit of injustice
and they turned their faces away and said
(Accompanied by chorus of PATIENTS.)

Our kingdom is not as the kingdom of this world
Our life on earth is but a pilgrimage
The soul lives on humility and patience
          (Continuing alone.)
at the same time screwing from the poor their last
     centime
They settled down among their treasures
and ate and drank with princes
and to the starving they said
          (Accompanied by chorus of PATIENTS.)
Suffer
Suffer as he suffered on the cross
for it is the will of God
          (A mime is performed. PATIENTS and
          the FOUR SINGERS come forward.
          Church dignitaries are depicted: CUCU-
          RUCU carries a cross made of brooms
          tied together and leads POLPOCH with a
          rope around his neck behind him. KOKOL
          swings a bucket as a censer. ROSSIGNOL
          counts her beads. Continuing alone.)
And anyone believes what they hear over and over
     again
so the poor instead of bread made do with a picture
of the bleeding scourged and nailed-up Christ
and prayed to that image of their helplessness
And the priests said
          (Accompanied by chorus of PATIENTS.
          The litanies of the SISTERS can also be
          heard.)
Raise your hands to heaven bend your knees
and bear your suffering without complaint
Pray for those who torture you
for prayer and blessing are the only stairways
which you can climb to Paradise
          (Speaking alone.)
And so they chained down the poor in their ignorance

so that they wouldn't stand up and fight their bosses
who ruled in the name of the lie of divine right

CHORUS

Amen

COULMIER
(Rising and calling above the Amen.)
Monsieur de Sade
I must interrupt this argument
We agreed to make some cuts in this passage
After all nobody now objects to the church
since our emperor is surrounded by high-ranking
      clergy
and since it's been proved over and over again
that the poor need the spiritual comfort of the
      priests
There's no question of anyone being oppressed
Quite on the contrary everything's done to relieve
      suffering
with clothing collections medical aid and soup
      kitchens
and in this very clinic we're dependent on the
      goodwill
not only of the temporal government
but even more on the goodness and understanding
      of the church

HERALD
(Raising his staff.)
If our performance causes aggravation
we hope you'll swallow down your indignation
and please remember that we show
only those things which happened long ago
Remember things were very different then
Of course today we're all God-fearing men
            (Makes the sign of the cross.)

14.   A REGRETTABLE INTERVENTION

> (A PATIENT, a clergyman's collar round
> his neck, detaches himself from the group
> and hops forward on his knees.)

PATIENT
(Stammering incoherently.)
Pray pray
O pray to him
Our Satan which art in hell
thy kingdom come
thy will be done
on earth as it is in hell
forgive us our good deeds
and deliver us from holiness
Lead us
Lead us into temptation
for ever and ever
        Amen

> (COULMIER has sprung to his feet. MALE
> NURSES throw themselves on the PA-
> TIENT, overpower him, put him under
> a shower, then bind him and drag him to
> the back.)

HERALD
(Swinging his rattle.)
The regrettable incident you've just seen
was unavoidable indeed foreseen
by our playwright who managed to compose
some extra lines in case the need arose
Please understand this man was once the very
well-thought-of abbot of a monastery
It should remind us all that as they say
God moves like man in a mysterious way

> (He swings his rattle. COULMIER sits

down.   The PATIENTS retreat and stretch
out on the benches, supervised by the
SISTERS and MALE NURSES.)

15.   CONTINUATION OF THE CONVERSATION
BETWEEN MARAT AND SADE

SADE
Before deciding what is wrong and what is right
first we must find out what we are
I
do not know myself
No sooner have I discovered something
than I begin to doubt it
and I have to destroy it again
What we do is just a shadow of what we want to do
and the only truths we can point to
are the ever-changing truths of our own experience
I do not know if I am hangman or victim
for I imagine the most horrible tortures
and as I describe them I suffer them myself
There is nothing that I could not do and everything
    fills me with horror
And I see that other people also
suddenly change themselves into strangers
and are driven to unpredictable acts
A little while ago I saw my tailor
a gentle cultured man who liked to talk philosophy
I saw him foam at the mouth
and raging and screaming attack with a cudgel
a man from Switzerland
a large man heavily armed
and destroy him utterly
and then I saw him
tear open the breast of the defeated man
saw him take out the still beating heart
and swallow it

(A PATIENT, in pacing across the stage
comes face to face with COULMIER and
addresses part of his speech directly to
him.)

PATIENT

A mad animal
Man's a mad animal
I'm a thousand years old and in my time
I've helped commit a million murders
The earth is spread
The earth is spread thick
with squashed human guts
We few survivors
We few survivors
walk over a quaking bog of corpses
always under our feet
every step we take
rotted bones ashes matted hair
under our feet
broken teeth skulls split open
A mad animal
I'm a mad animal
            (SADE comes up to him and leads him
            gently to the back as he continues.)
Prisons don't help
Chains don't help
I escape
through all the walls
through all the shit and the splintered bones
You'll see it all one day
I'm not through yet
I have plans
            (MARAT searches for his cue.)

HERALD
(Prompting.)

O this itching

MARAT

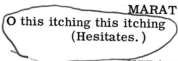

O this itching this itching
(Hesitates.)

HERALD
(Prompting.)
This fever

MARAT

This fever beats in my head like a drum
my skin simmers and scorches
Simonne
Simonne dip the cloth in vinegar and water
cool my forehead

(SIMONNE hastens to him and goes through
her motions.)

SADE

Marat I know
that you'd give up your fame and all the love of the
people
for a few days of health
You lie in your bath
as if you were in the pink water of the womb
You swim all huddled up
alone with your ideas about the world
which no longer fit the world outside
And why should you care about the world outside
For me the only reality is imagination
the world inside myself
The Revolution
no longer interests me

MARAT

Wrong Sade wrong

No restless ideas
can break down the walls
I never believed the pen alone
could destroy institutions
However hard we try to bring in the new
it comes into being only
in the midst of clumsy deals
We're all so clogged with dead ideas
passed from generation to generation
that even the best of us
don't know the way out
We invented the Revolution
but we don't know how to run it
Look everyone wants to keep something from the
        past
a souvenir of the old regime
        This man decides to keep a painting
        This one keeps his mistress
        This man keeps his horse
        He (pointing) keeps his garden
        He (pointing) keeps his estate
        He keeps his country house
        He keeps his factories
        This man couldn't part with his shipyards
        This one kept his army
        and that one keeps his king
And so we stand here
and write into the declaration of the rights of man
the holy right of property
And now we find where that leads
Every man's equally free to fight
fraternally and with equal arms of course
Every man his own millionaire
Man against man group against group
in happy mutual robbery
                (The PATIENTS stand up slowly, some
                step forward. The SINGERS take up

their positions.)
And ahead of them the great springtime of mankind
the budding of trade and the blossoming of industry
and one enormous financial upsurge
We stand here more oppressed than when we begun
(Points across the auditorium.)
and they think that the revolution's been won

16.   THE PEOPLE'S REACTION

/The People's Reaction/

THE FOUR SINGERS
(With musical accompaniment.)
Why do they have the gold
Why do they have all the power
Why do they have friends at the top
Why do they have jobs at the top
We've got nothing always had nothing
nothing but holes and millions of them

KOKOL

Living in holes

POLPOCH

Dying in holes

CUCURUCU
Holes in our bellies

ROSSIGNOL
and holes in our clothes

/Marat We're Poor/
(Reprise)

THE FOUR SINGERS and CHORUS
Marat we're poor and the poor stay poor

Marat don't make us wait any more
We want our rights and we don't care how
We want our Revolution *now*.

                    HERALD
          (Coming forward quickly, swinging his
          staff. Music ends. The FOUR SINGERS
          and CHORUS withdraw.)
Observe how easily a crowd turns mob
through ingnorance of its wise ruler's job
Rather than bang an empty drum
of protest citizens be dumb
Work for and trust the powerful few
what's best for them is best for you
Ladies and gentlemen we'd like to see
people and government in harmony
a harmony which I should say
we've very nearly reached today
          (DUPERRET and the SISTERS busy them-
          selves with CORDAY, who cannot be awak-
          ened. They pull her to her feet and hold
          her up and try to get her moving.)

17. FIRST CONVERSATION BETWEEN CORDAY
     AND DUPERRET

          (CORDAY is led forward by the two SIS-
          TERS, supporting her under the arms.
          DUPERRET walks behind supporting Cor-
          day's back with his hands.)

                    HERALD
          (Plays a few runs on his Pan-flute.)
And now nobility meets grace
Our author brings them face to face
The beautiful and brave Charlotte Corday
          (Turns round in concern, nods in relief

              and points his staff at CORDAY.)
The handsome Monsieur Duperret
              (With the help of the SISTERS, CORDAY
              enters the arena. DUPERRET walks be-
              side her. The SISTERS withdraw. COR-
              DAY and DUPERRET greet each other
              with exaggerated ceremony.)
In Caen where she spent the best years of her youth
in a convent devoted to the way of truth
Duperret's name she heard them recommend
as a most sympathetic helpful friend
              (DUPERRET uses the scene to make amo-
              rous advances to CORDAY. The HERALD
              addresses DUPERRET.)
Confine your passion to the lady's mind
Your love's platonic not the other kind
              (He gives the Orchestra a sign with his
              staff. CORDAY stands with head held
              back, eyes closed. The Orchestra plays
              the Corday theme. The HERALD with-
              draws. He waits a few seconds and watch-
              es CORDAY.)

                    CORDAY
              (With her eyes closed.)
Ah dearest Duperret
              (She hesitates then starts again as if sing-
              ing an aria.)
Ah dearest Duperret what can we do
How can we stop this dreadful calamity
In the streets everyone is saying
Marat's to be
              (She hesitates. DUPERRET gently caress-
              es her hips and back.)
Marat's to be tribune and dictator
He still pretends that his iron grip
will relax as soon as the worst is over

But we know what Marat really wants
anarchy and confusion
       (CORDAY stands sunk into herself.)

           DUPERRET
       (Embracing CORDAY, also as if singing
       an aria, but with great ardour.)
Dearest Charlotte you must return
return to your friends the pious nuns
and live in prayer and contemplation
You cannot fight
the hard-faced enemies surrounding us
       (One of the SISTERS approaches DUPER-
       RET and pulls back his hand, which he
       had placed on her bosom. CORDAY stands
       sunk into herself.)
You talk about Marat but who's this Marat
A street salesman a funfair barker
a layabout from Corsica sorry I mean Sardinia
Marat the name sounds Jewish to me
perhaps derived from the waters of Marah in the
    Bible
But who listens to him
Only the mob down in the streets
Up here Marat can be no danger to us
       (DUPERRET embraces Corday's hips.
       The FOUR SINGERS are filling in time
       with all sorts of pranks, throwing dice
       and showing each other card tricks.)

           CORDAY
       (Suddenly awake and full of power.)
Dearest Duperret you're trying to test me
but I know what I must do
       (Tries to free herself from Duperret's
       embrace.   The two SISTERS standing
       behind the podium interfere and pull back

                    Duperret's hands.)
Duperret go to Caen
Barbaroux and Buzot are waiting for you there
Go now and travel quickly
Do not wait till this evening
for this evening everything will be too late

                        DUPERRET
                (Passionately, in aria style as before.)
Dearest Charlotte my place is here
                (Throws himself on his knees and hugs
                her legs.)
How could I leave the city which holds you
Dearest Charlotte
my place is here
                (He forgets himself and becomes wilder
                in his embracing. The HERALD pushes
                him with his staff and then taps on the
                floor.)

                        HERALD
                (Prompting.)
And why should I run

                        DUPERRET
And why should I run
now when it can't last much longer
                (Stroking CORDAY vigorously.)
Already the English lie off Dunkirk and Toulon
The Prussians

                        HERALD
                (Prompting.)
The Spaniards

                        DUPERRET
The Spaniards have occupied Roussillon

Paris

HERALD
(Prompting.)
Mayence

DUPERRET
Mayence is surrounded by the Prussians
Condé and Valenciennes have fallen to the English

HERALD
(Correcting.)
Austrians

DUPERRET
To the Austrians
The Vendée is up in arms
>   (With much ardour and vigorous embrac-
>   es.)
They can't hold out much longer
these fanatical upstarts
with no vision and no culture
They can't hold out much longer
No dear Charlotte here I stay
>   (Snuggles up to her and puts his head in-
>   to her lap.)
waiting for the promised day
when with Marat's mob interred
France once more speaks the forbidden word
Freedom
>   (DUPERRET raises himself, clinging to
>   CORDAY, tries to kiss her. CORDAY ex-
>   tricates herself, the two SISTERS come
>   to her aid, pushing DUPERRET away and
>   pulling her back to her bench. The music
>   ends.)

18.   SADE TURNS HIS BACK ON ALL THE NATIONS

SADE
(Shouting to MARAT.)
You hear that Marat
Freedom
They all say they want what's best for France
My patriotism's bigger than yours
They're all ready to die for the honour of France
Radical or moderate
they're all after the taste of blood
(Rising.)
The luke-warm liberals and the angry radicals
all believe in the greatness of France
Marat
can't you see this patriotism is lunacy
·Long ago I left heroics to the heroes
and I care no more for this country
than for any other country

COULMIER
(Calling over them with raised forefinger.)
Take care

PATIENT
(In the background.)
Long live Napoleon and the nation
(A shrill laugh in the background.)

KOKOL

(At back calling.)
Long live all emperors kings bishops and popes
(Signs of disorder in the background.)

POLPOCH
Long live watery broth and the straitjacket

ROSSIGNOL

Long live Marat

ROUX

Long live the Revolution
(Shouting above the disorder.)

SADE

It's easy to get mass movements going
movements that move in vicious circles
(Shrill whistles in background. A PA-
TIENT begins to run in a circle, a second
and third join in. MALE NURSES pursue
them and halt them.)

SADE

I don't believe in idealists
who charge down blind alleys
I don't believe in any of the sacrifices
that have been made for any cause
I believe only in myself

MARAT
(Turning violently to SADE.)
I believe only in that thing which you betray
We've overthrown our wealthy rabble of rulers
disarmed many of them though
many escaped
But now those rulers have been replaced by others
who used to carry torches and banners with us
and now long for the good old days
It becomes clear
that the Revolution was fought
for merchants and shopkeepers
the bourgeoisie
a new victorious class
and underneath them

ourselves
who always lose the lottery

[Those Fat Monkeys]

FOUR SINGERS
Those fat monkeys covered in banknotes
have champagne and brandy on tap
They're up to their eyeballs in franc notes
We're up to our noses in crap

Those gorilla-mouthed fakers
are longing to see us all rot
The gentry may lose a few acres
but we lose the little we've got

Revolution it's more like a ruin
They're all stuffed with glorious food
They think about nothing but screwing
but we are the ones who get screwed

19.) FIRST RABBLE-ROUSING OF JACQUES ROUX

ROUX
(Springing on a bench in background, shout-
ing.)
Pick up your arms
Fight for your rights
Grab what you need and grab it now
or wait a hundred years
and see what the authorities arrange
(PATIENTS approach ROUX from the tri-
bunal.)
Up there they despise you
because you never had the cash
to learn to read and write
You're good enough for the dirty work of the

Revolution
but they screw their noses up at you
because your sweat stinks
You have to sit way down there
so they won't have to see you
And down there
in ignorance and stink
you're allowed to do your bit
toward bringing in the golden age
in which you'll all do the same old dirty work
Up there in the sunlight
their poets sing
about the power of life
and the expensive rooms in which they scheme
are hung with exquisite paintings
So stand up
Defend yourselves from their whips
Stand up stand in front of them
and let them see how many of you there are
> (The FOUR SINGERS sit down in the
> arena and pass a bottle around. The
> two SISTERS grab ROUX from behind
> and pull him down from the dais.)

COULMIER
(Springing up.)
Do we have to listen to this sort of thing
We're citizens of a new enlightened age
We're all revolutionaries nowadays
but this is plain treachery we can't allow it

HERALD
(Sounding a shrill whistle.)
The cleric you've been listening to
is that notorious priest Jacques Roux
> (Points with his staff at ROUX.)
who to adopt the new religious fashion

has quit the pulpit and with earthier passion
rages from soapboxes A well-trained priest
his rhetoric is slick to say the least
'If you'd make paradise your only chance
is not to build on clouds but solid France'
The mob eats from his hand while Roux
knows what he wants but not what he should do
Talk's cheap The price of action is colossal
so Roux decides to be the chief apostle
of Jean-Paul Marat Seems good policy
since Marat's heading straight for Calvary
and crucifixion all good Christians know
is the most sympathetic way to go

                    ROUX
            (Frees himself and jumps forward)
We demand
the opening of the granaries to feed the poor
We demand
the public ownership of workshops and factories
                    (The FOUR SINGERS listen to the disturb-
                    ance, but soon lose interest.   They quar-
                    rel for the last drop of the bottle.)
We demand
the conversion of the churches into schools
so that now at last something useful can be taught
    in them
                    (COULMIER wrings his hands and signi-
                    fies protest.)
We demand that everyone should do all they can
to put an end to war
This damned war
which is run for the benefit of profiteers
and leads only to more wars
                    (COULMIER runs across to SADE and
                    speaks to him, but SADE does not react.)
We demand

that the people who started the war
should pay the cost of it
                    (The FOUR SINGERS continue their an-
                    tics.)
Once and for all
the idea of glorious victories
won by the glorious army
must be wiped out
Neither side is glorious
On either side they're just frightened men messing
      their pants
and they all want the same thing
Not to lie under the earth
but to walk upon it
without crutches

                         COULMIER
                    (Shouting over him.)
This is outright defeatism
At this very moment our soldiers are laying down
      their lives
for the freedom of the world and for our freedom
                    (Turning violently to SADE.)
This scene was cut

                           SADE
                    (Calling out, without concerning himself
                    with Coulmier's protest.)
Bravo Jacques Roux
I like your monk's habit
Nowadays it's best
to preach revolution
wearing a robe
                    (ROUX is overpowered by the two NURSES
                    and dragged off. DUPERRET makes vio-
                    lent passes at CORDAY, who remains im-
                    passive. The PATIENTS come forward

restlessly.)

ROUX
(As he is being strapped to a bench.)

Marat
Your hour has come
Now Marat show yourself
Come out and lead the people
They are waiting for you
It must be now
For the Revolution
which burns up everything
in blinding brightness
will only last as long as a lightning flash

20. MONSIEUR DE SADE IS WHIPPED

(ROUX jumps up, the bench strapped to
his back. He is overpowered. The PA-
TIENTS are pushed back. SADE comes
slowly into the arena. He speaks without bothering about the noise.)

SADE

Marat
Today they need you because you are going to
    suffer for them
They need you and they honour the urn which holds
    your ashes
Tomorrow they will come back and smash that urn
and they will ask
Marat who was Marat
Marat
Now I will tell you
what I think of this revolution
which I helped to make
                (It has become very quiet in the back-

          ground.)
When I lay in the Bastille
my ideas were already formed
I sweated them out
under the blows of my own whip
out of hatred for myself
and the limitations of my mind
In prison I created in my mind
monstrous representatives of a dying class
who could only exercise their power
in spectacularly staged orgies
I recorded the mechanics of their atrocities
in the minutest detail
and brought out everything wicked and brutal
that lay inside me
In a criminal society
I dug the criminal out of myself
so I could understand him and so understand
the times we live in
My imaginary giants committed
desecrations and tortures
I committed them myself
and like them allowed myself to be bound and beatei
And even now I should like to take
this beauty here
          (Pointing to CORDAY, who is brought
          forward.)
who stands there so expectantly
and let her beat me
while I talk to you about the Revolution
          (The SISTERS place CORDAY in the
          arena. SADE hands her a many-stranded
          whip.   He tears off his shirt and offers
          his back to CORDAY. He stands facing
          the audience.   CORDAY stands behind
          him.   The PATIENTS advance slowly
          from the background.   The ladies on

Coulmier's dais stand up expectantly.)
At first I saw in the revolution a chance
for a tremendous outburst of revenge
an orgy greater than all my dreams
            (CORDAY slowly raises the whip and
            lashes him. SADE cowers.)
But then I saw
when I sat in the courtroom myself
            (Whiplash. SADE gasps.)
not as I had been before the accused
but as a judge
I couldn't bring myself
to deliver the prisoners to the hangman
            (Whiplash.)
I did all I could to release them or let them escape
I saw I wasn't capable of murder
            (Whiplash. SADE groans asthmatically.)
although murder
was the final proof of my existence
and now
            (Whiplash. He gasps and groans.)
the very thought of it
horrifies me
In September when I saw
the official sacking of the Carmelite Convent
I had to bend over in the courtyard
and vomit
            (CORDAY stops, herself breathing heav-
            ily.)
as I saw my own prophecies coming true
            (He falls down on his knees. CORDAY
            stands before him.)
and women running by
holding in their dripping hands
the severed genitals of men
            (CORDAY flogs him again. He groans
            and falls forward.)

And then in the next few months
          (Hindered by his asthma.)
as the tumbrels ran regularly to the scaffolds
and the blade dropped and was winched up and
     dropped again
          (Whiplash.)
all the meaning drained out of this revenge
It had become mechanical
               (Another blow. He crumples.   CORDAY
               stands very erect.)
It was inhuman it was dull
and curiously technocratic
          (Whiplash.)
And now Marat
          (Whiplash.   SADE breathes heavily.)
now I see where
this revolution is leading
               (CORDAY stands breathlessly, holding
               the whip over SADE. The two SISTERS
               move forward and pull her back.   She
               does not resist, dragging the whip be-
               hind her. SADE continues, lying on his
               knees.)
To the withering of the individual man
and a slow merging into uniformity
to the death of choice
to self denial
to deadly weakness
in a state
which has no contact with individuals
but which is impregnable
So I turn away
I am one of those who has to be defeated
and from this defeat I want to seize
all I can get with my own strength
I step out of my place
and watch what happens

without joining in
observing
noting down my observations
and all around me
stillness
          (Pauses, breathing heavily.)
And when I vanish
I want all trace of my existence
to be wiped out
          (He takes his shirt and returns to his
          chair, slowly dressing.)

21. POOR OLD MARAT

                MARAT
          (Bent forward, sunk into himself.)
Simonne Simonne
          (Staring as if blind.)
Why is it getting so dark
Give me a fresh cloth for my forehead
Put a new towel round my shoulders
I don't know
if I am freezing or burning to death
          (SIMONNE stands ready and bends over
          him with her jerky movements, puts a
          hand to his brow, changes the cloths,
          fans him. The PATIENTS cower behind
          the arena.)
Simonne
Fetch Bas so I can dictate my call
my call to the people of France
          (SIMONNE shakes her head in horror and
          puts a hand over her mouth.)
Simonne
Where are my papers
I saw them only a moment ago
Why is it so dark

SIMONNE
(Pushing the papers lying on the board
nearer.)
They're here can't you see Jean-Paul

MARAT

Where's the ink
Where's my pen

SIMONNE
(Indicating.)
Here's your pen Jean-Paul
and here's the ink
where it always is
That was only a cloud over the sun
or perhaps smoke
They are burning the corpses
(The orchestra plays. The FOUR SING-
ERS come forward.)

[Poor Old Marat]

FOUR SINGERS
(Singing to music.)
Poor old Marat they hunt you down
The blood hounds are sniffing all over the town
Just yesterday your printing press
was smashed Now they're asking your home
    address

Poor old Marat in you we trust
You work till your eyes turn as red as rust
but while you write they're on your track
The boots mount the staircase the door's flung
    back
(Together with CHORUS.)

[Marat We're Poor]

FOUR SINGERS
Marat we're poor and the poor stay poor
Marat don't make us wait any more
We want our rights and we don't care how
We want our Revolution *now.*
>   (Music finale. SINGERS withdraw. The
>   PATIENTS close the curtain.)

22. SECOND CONVERSATION BETWEEN CORDAY
AND DUPERRET

>   (The SISTERS and DUPERRET busy them-
>   selves with CORDAY. Together they raise
>   her up. The SISTERS arrange her clothes
>   and tie on her hat. The HERALD comes
>   forward and knocks his staff on the floor
>   three times.)

HERALD
>   (Plays a few runs on his Pan-flute.)
Now that these painful matters have been clarified
let's turn and look upon the sunny side
Fever sores blows not one of them destroys
the universal rule of love's sweet joys
Anger and woe don't give a true reflection
of life there's also spiritual affection
Recall this couple and their love so pure
>   (CORDAY is led to the center by SISTERS.
>   DUPERRET has his arm around her. The
>   HERALD points his staff.)
she with her neatly-groomed coiffure
>   (Points to it.)
and her face intriguingly pale and clear
>   (Points to it.)
and her eyes ashine with the trace of a tear

(Points to them.)
her lips sensual and ripe seeming to silently cry
    for protection
            (Points to them.)
and his embraces proving his affection
            (Points to DUPERRET, who lifts Corday's
            foot and kisses her shoe, then covers her
            leg in kisses. CORDAY pushes him back.)
See how he moves with natural grace
            (DUPERRET loses his balance and, with-
            out grace, sits on his behind, but rises
            immediately and strikes a comic amorous
            pose before CORDAY, who turns her face
            from him in disgust.)
and how his heart sprints on at passion's pace
            (Points to Duperret's breast.)
Let's gaze at the sweet blending of the strong and
    fair sex
before their heads fall off their necks
            (Orchestra plays Corday theme. She hes-
            itates, looking for her words. The HER-
            ALD prompts her.)

[One Day It Will Come to Pass]

HERALD
One day it will come to pass

CORDAY
(In the aria style.)
One day it will come to pass
Man will live in harmony with himself
and with his fellow-man

DUPERRET
(Covers her hand and arm with kisses.)
One day it will come

(He strokes her hair, singing in the aria
style.)
a society which will pool its energy
to defend and protect
each person for the possession of each person
and in which each individual
although united with all the others
(Putting a hand under Corday's dress.
She defends herself.)
only obeys himself
and so stays free
(DUPERRET tries to kiss Corday's mouth.
She avoids him.)

CORDAY

A society
in which every man is trusted with the right
of governing himself himself

DUPERRET

(Holding CORDAY and embracing her violently.)
One day it will come
a constitution in which the natural inequalities of
    man
(CORDAY leans back. DUPERRET jumps
after her, continuing.)
are subject to a higher order
(Breathless.)
so that all
(One of the SISTERS gets hold of CORDAY
and leads her back. CORDAY is placed in
a heroic pose.)
however varied their physical and mental powers
    may be
by agreement legally
get their fair share

(He utters a sigh of relief, and then he
also falls into a suitable pose so that they
form a pleasant tableau.)

23.   THESE LIES THEY TELL

(MARAT raises himself up.   CORDAY is
led back by the SISTERS.   DUPERRET
follows her.)

MARAT

These lies they tell about the ideal state
The rich will never give away their property
of their own free will
And if by force of circumstances
they have to give up just a little
here and there
they do it only because they know
they'll soon win it back again
The rumour spreads
that the workers can soon expect higher wages
Why

(The head of a PATIENT appears from
behind the curtain, which is opened from
inside.)

Because this raises production and increases
    demand
to fill the rich man's gold-chest
Don't imagine
that you can beat them without using force

(The PATIENTS rise one by one and ad-
vance slowly, listening intently. CORDAY
lies stretched out on the dais, DUPERRET
leans over her.)

Don't be deceived
when our Revolution has been finally stamped out
and they tell you

things are better now
Even if there's no poverty to be seen
because the poverty's been hidden
even if you ever got more wages
and could afford to buy
more of these new and useless goods
which these new industries foist on you
and even if it seems to you
that you never had so much
that is only the slogan of those
who still have much more than you
            (The PATIENTS and FOUR SINGERS ad-
            vance slowly.)
Don't be taken in
when they pat you paternally on the shoulder and
      say
that there's no inequality worth speaking of
and no more reason
for fighting
            (COULMIER looks around, worried.)
Because if you believe them
            (Turns toward the audience.)
they will be completely in charge
in their marble homes and granite banks
from which they rob the people of the world
under the pretence of bringing them culture
            (COULMIER leaves the platform and
            hurries toward SADE. He speaks to
            him.   SADE does not react.)
Watch out
for as soon as it pleases them
they'll send you out
to protect their gold
in wars
            (SADE rises and moves to the arena.)
whose weapons rapidly developed
by servile scientists

will become more and more deadly
until they can with a flick of a finger
tear a million of you to pieces

SADE

Lying there
scratched and swollen
your brow burning
> (COULMIER nods with satisfaction and
> returns to the platform.)

in your world your bath
you still believe that justice is possible
you still believe all men are equal
Do you still believe that all occupations
are equally valuable equally satisfying
and that no man wants to be greater than the others
How does the old song go

24. SONG AND MIME OF THE GLORIFICATION OF THE BENEFICIARY

> (The FOUR SINGERS perform a mime,
> in which they illustrate the cash value
> of all the things SADE names.)

SADE

One always bakes the most delicate cakes
Two is the really superb masseur
Three sets your hair with exceptional flair
Four's brandy goes to the Emperor
Five knows each trick of advanced rhetoric
Six bred a beautiful brand-new rose
Seven can cook every dish in the book
And eight cuts you flawlessly elegant clothes
Do you think those eight would be happy
if each of them could climb so high
and no higher

before banging their heads on equality
if each could be only a small link
in a long and heavy chain
Do you still think it's possible
to unite mankind
when already you see how the few idealists
who did join together in the name of harmony
are now out of tune
and would like to kill each other over trifles

                    MARAT
               (Raising himself.)
But they aren't trifles
They are matters of principle
and it's usual in a revolution
for the half-hearted and the fellow-travellers
to be dropped
                    (Mime ends. MARAT stands up in the
                    bath.)
We can't begin to build till we've burnt the old
     building down
however dreadful that may seem to those
who lounge in make-believe contentment
wearing their scruples as protective clothing
Listen
Can you hear through the walls
how they plot and whisper
                    (MARAT gets out of the bath and stum-
                    bles around the arena as if about to faint.
                    Some nurses seize him and put him back
                    into the bath.)
Do you see how they lurk everywhere
waiting for the chance to strike

                    THE FOUR SINGERS
                    (To music accompaniment, singly, speak-
                    ing in conversational tones while prome-

nading.)
What has gone wrong with
the men who are ruling
I'd like to know who
they think they are fooling
They told us that torture
was over and gone
but everyone knows
the same torture goes on
The king's gone away
The priests emigrating
The nobles are buried
so why are we waiting

25. CORDAY'S SECOND VISIT

(CORDAY is prepared by the SISTERS,
who lead her forward. DUPERRET follows them. MARAT sits waiting in his
bath. SIMONNE changes his cloths. SADE
stands in front of his chair. CORDAY is
placed on the arena in a pose. She holds
up her hand as if about to knock. The
SISTERS stand behind her ready to support
her. DUPERRET sits down. The FOUR
SINGERS stop in front of the musicians.
The HERALD gives CORDAY a sign with
his staff, she moves her hand as if knocking, and the HERALD knocks three times
with his staff on the floor. The orchestra
plays the Corday theme.)

HERALD
Now Charlotte Corday stands outside
Marat's front door the second time she's tried
(Points to CORDAY. SIMONNE straight-
ens and goes a few steps toward COR-

DAY.)

CORDAY
(Quietly.)
I have come
to deliver this letter
(Draws a letter from her bodice.)
in which I ask again
to be received by Marat
(Hesitates.)
I am unhappy
and therefore have a right to his aid
(CORDAY holds the letter out to SIMONNE.
SIMONNE, confused, takes a step toward
CORDAY, returns to the back and begins
to change Marat's bandage.)

CORDAY
(Repeating loudly.)
I have a right to his aid
(She stretches out her hand. SIMONNE
wavers nervously about, then runs to
CORDAY and snatches the letter from
her.)

MARAT
Who was that at the door Simonne
(SIMONNE hesitates in confusion between
CORDAY and MARAT.)

HERALD
(Prompting.)
A girl from Caen with a letter
a petitioner
(CORDAY is now standing sunk into herself. DUPERRET rises and puts his arm
around her waist. The two SISTERS come

up.   CORDAY is led off.)

SIMONNE
(Confused and angry.)
I won't let anyone in
They only bring us trouble
All these people with their convulsions and
    complaints
As if you had nothing better to do
than be their lawyer and doctor and confessor
            (She tears the letter up and puts the piec-
            es in her apron. She puts a fresh cloth
            around Marat's shoulders.)

SADE
(Goes into the arena and stops near the
bath. Musical accompaniment.)
That's how it is Marat
That's how she sees your revolution
They have toothache
and their teeth should be pulled
            (The FOUR SINGERS mime the charac-
            ters in his speech. They mime very slow-
            ly, with economical gestures illustrating
            suffering.)
Their soup's burnt
They shout for better soup
A woman finds her husband too short
she wants a taller one
A man finds his wife too skinny
he wants a plumper one
A man's shoes pinch
but his neighbour's shoes fit comfortably
A poet runs out of poetry
and desperately gropes for new images
For hours an angler casts his line
Why aren't the fish biting

And so they join the revolution
thinking the revolution will give them everything
a fish
a poem
a new pair of shoes
a new wife
a new husband
and the best soup in the world
So they storm all the citadels
and there they are
and everything is just the same
no fish biting
verses botched
shoes pinching
a worn and stinking partner in bed
and the soup burnt
and all that heroism
which drove us down to the sewers
well we can talk about it to our grandchildren
if we have any grandchildren
>   (Music changes to a quartet with tragic
>   flavour.)

>   THE FOUR SINGERS
>   (Taking up their positions.)
Marat Marat it's all in vain
You studied the body and probed the brain
In vain you spent your energies
for how can Marat cure his own disease

Marat Marat where is our path
or is it not visible from your bath
Your enemies are closing in
Without you the people can never win
>   (MARAT lays himself wearily across
>   the board.)
Marat Marat can you explain

how once in the daylight your thought seemed plain
Has your affliction left you dumb
Your thoughts lie in shadows now night has come
> (The music changes to a dramatic growl-
> ing.   MARAT is in a fever.   SIMONNE
> feels his brow, fans him, changes his
> bandage.)

26.   THE FACES OF MARAT

> (The whole stage trembles and roars.
> The mimes appear with a cart.   The cart
> is drawn by a man and a woman who repre-
> sent Marat's parents. The characters in
> the cart stand for Science, the Army, the
> Church, the Nouveaux Riches. The priest
> blesses the owner of the sack of gold loot-
> ed from the aristocrats.   The figures are
> bedecked with medals and with primitive
> insignia.   The costumes are extremely
> grotesque.)

MARAT
(Raising himself up.)
They are coming
Listen to them
and look carefully at
these gathering figures
Listen closely
Watch
Yes I hear you
all the voices I ever heard
Yes I see you
all the old faces
> (The loud noise continues.)

HERALD
(Tapping his staff.)

Ladies and gentlemen silence I pray
Let's hear what these people are aching to say
          (Pointing to figures.)
about this man
          (Pointing to MARAT.)
whom they all understood
before they bury him for good
First the schoolmaster of that charming place
          (Points to SCHOOLMASTER.)
in which this man
          (Points to MARAT.)
spent his childhood days

SCHOOLMASTER
          (Sings in a falsetto voice.)
Even as a child
this Marat
made groups of his friends
rush screaming at each other
they fought with wooden swords
but real blood flowed
          (Cries are heard in the background.)
and they took prisoners
and bound and tortured them
and nobody knew why

HERALD
          (Pointing to the figure representing
          Marat's mother.)
Now let us hear this lady for she can
give us the inside story of this man
She smelt him from the very first
for from her womb young Marat burst

MOTHER
          (In a complaining voice.)
Wouldn't eat his food

Lay around for days saying nothing
Broke a lot of canes on his hide we did
>   (She laughs shrilly. Laughter is heard
>   in the background, also the sound of
>   whipping.)

Locked him up in the cellar of course
but nothing helped
There was no getting at him
Oh
>   (She starts laughing again.)

FATHER
>   (Springing forward, in a hurried voice.)

When I bit him he bit back
his own father
Threw himself down when I wanted to hang him up
and when I spat at him he lay there stiff as a
   poker
cold as ice
>   (Starts to laugh harshly.)

MARAT

Yes I see you
hated father hated mother
>   (The two figures squat down, still shak-
>   ing with laughter. They rock to and fro
>   as if sitting in a boat.)

What's that boat you're rocking in
I see you
I hear you
Why do you laugh like executioners
>   (The two figures sit rocking, their laugh-
>   ter dies.)

SIMONNE
>   (Approaching the bath.)

Jean-Paul you're feverish

Stop writing Jean-Paul
or it'll kill you
Lie still
You must take more care of yourself

MARAT
I'm not feverish
Now I see clearly
those figures were always hallucinations
Why doesn't Bas come
Fetch him
My call to the nation
I must write my call
Bas

SCHOOLMASTER
(Jumping forward.)
When he was five this loudmouth boasted
I can do anything teacher can do
and what's more I know more
and at fifteen I've conquered the uni-v-v-v-
    versities
and outdone all the p-p-professors
and at the age of twenty I've mastered
the entire in-in-in-intellectual cosmos
That's what he boasted
as true as I stand here
            (Swings his cane.)

MARAT
Simonne
where are my old manuscripts
My novel about the young Count Potovsky
and my book about the chains of slavery

SIMONNE
(Defensively.)

Leave all that stuff
It'll only bring you trouble

MARAT
(Raising himself up.)
I want to see them
Look for them
bring them to me

SCHOOLMASTER
Scribblings of a pickpocket
pilfered thoughts
frivolities tirades

MILITARY REPRESENTATIVE
One book published under the name of a count
The other under the name of a prince
Just look at him
this charlatan
greedy for titles and court distinctions
who turned on those he once flattered
only because they did not recognize him

A SCIENTIST
What did he do in England this shady Marat
Wasn't he a dandy in the highest society
who had to run away
because he was caught red-handed embezzling
    and stealing
Didn't he smuggle himself back into well-known
    circles
and get himself appointed physician
to the Count d'Artois
or was it only to his horses
Didn't we see him going about with aristocrats
He charged thirty-six livres for a consultation
and on top of that enjoyed the favours of

certain well-born ladies
                    (COULMIER'S wife and daughter applaud.)

A NEWLY RICH
And when at last they let him drop
back to his kind the simple poor
and when he spoke and couldn't stop
each word from branding him a boor
and when they found he was a quack
with watered drugs and pills of chalk
and when they threw him on his back
He raised his battered head to squawk
      Property is Robbery
                    (Cries in the background.)
      Down with all Tyrants
                    (The cry is taken up in the background.)

MARAT
Bas fetch Bas
                    (VOLTAIRE emerges from the darkness,
                    suitably masked and with corkscrew curls.)

CHORUS
Bas

HERALD
            (As VOLTAIRE advances.)
It is a privilege indeed
to introduce Voltaire He wrote Candide

VOLTAIRE
            (Monotonously.)
We have received from a certain Marat
a slim volume
entitled Man
This Marat claims in a somewhat revolutionary
      essay

that the soul exists in the walls of the brain
and from that strategic point controls
the hypodraulic mechanism of the body
by means of a network of tinkling nerve threads
At the same time apparently the soul is receiving
messages from the mechanamism of the body
messages conveyed by pistons plugs and wires
which the soul transforms into consciousness
    through separate
centimentrifuges operating asimultaneously
In other words
it is the opinion of this gentleman
that a corn fills the corridors of the brain with
    pain of the soul
and that a troubled soul curdles the liver and kidneys
For this kind of ring-a-ring-a-roses
we can spare not even our laughter
            (CUCURUCU and ROSSIGNOL laugh iron-
            ically Ha Ha Ha. A figure with a palm
            branch moves forward.)

HERALD
We're equally happy to welcome today
that eminent scientist Lavoisier
        (Points to him.)

LAVOISIER
        (Monotonously.)
The Academy has received from a certain Marat
some theories concerning fire light and electricity
This Marat seems entirely certain
that he knows a great deal better than the Academy
For fire he says is not an element
but a liquid fluidium caused by heat
which only ignites because of air
Light he proceeds to say is not light
but a path of vibratorating rays
left behind by light

Certainly an extraordinary scientist
He goes further
Heat according to him is not of course heat
but simply more vibratoratory rays
which become heat only
when they collide with a body and set in motion-
        ability
its minuscule molecules
He wants to pronounce
the whole of firm and fixed creation
invalid
And instead he wants to introduce
a universe of unbridled activation
in which electrified magnetic forces
whizz about and rub against each other
No wonder that the author sits there in his bath
attempting to determine the validity of the proposition
The more you scratch the more you itch

        (KOKOL and POLPOCH laugh ironically
        Ha Ha Ha. FATHER and MOTHER join
        in the laughter. The figures mime the
        attitude of judges about to give a verdict.)

VOLTAIRE
So this frustrated Newton's eyes

PRIEST
turned to the streets He thought it best

SCHOOLMASTER
to join the revolutionaries

NEWLY RICH
and beat his dilettante breast

PRIEST
crying out The oppressed must rise

LAVOISIER

He meant of course I am oppressed
> (Rocking to and fro and laughing, the
> FATHER and MOTHER pull back the
> cart with the figures. ROUX hurries
> to the front, a belated advocate.)

ROUX

Woe to the man who is different
who tries to break down all the barriers
Woe to the man
who tries to stretch the imagination of man
He shall be mocked he shall be scourged
by the blinkered guardians of morality
You wanted enlightenment and warmth
and so you studied light and heat
> (Unrest in background.)

You wondered how forces can be controlled
so you studied electricity
You wanted to know what man is for
so you asked yourself What is this soul
this dump for hollow ideals and mangled morals
You decided that the soul is in the brain
> (The PATIENTS form into a group and
> advance.)

and that it can learn to think
For to you the soul is a practical thing
a tool for ruling and mastering life
And you came one day to the Revolution
because you saw the most important vision
That our circumstances must be changed
    fundamentally
and without these changes
everything we try to do must fail
> (COULMIER jumps up. The SISTERS
> and MALE NURSES run toward ROUX
> and pull him into the background. SADE

(stands erect in front of his chair and
smiles. CORDAY lies sleeping on her
bench. DUPERRET sits by her on the
floor.)

[Marat We're Poor]

CHORUS
(To music while the SISTERS sing a
litany.)
Marat we're poor and the poor stay poor
Marat don't make us wait any more
We want our rights and we don't care how
We want our Revolution *now*.
(Music ends.)

HERALD
(Swinging his rattle.)
The end comes soon Before we watch the crime
let's interpose a drinking thinking time
while you recall that what our cast presents
is simply this a series of events
but that our end which might seem prearranged
could be delayed or even changed
We will since it's a play not actual history
postpone it with an interval We guarantee
that after your refreshments and debating
you'll find Marat still in his bathtub waiting
(Points to MARAT.)

CURTAIN

ACT TWO

The handbell is rung behind the curtain.   Curtain
goes up.

27.   THE NATIONAL ASSEMBLY

The setting is the same, but with the following
changes: DUPERRET sits on the steps leading to
Sade's raised chair, between the two PATIENTS
representing prostitutes.   On the left are seated
the PATIENTS who represent the Girondists
in the National Assembly.

SADE stands underneath Coulmier's platform.
The bath has been removed from Marat's dais.
On it are the FOUR SINGERS and the PATIENTS
who represent the Jacobites. PATIENTS sit on
benches alongside the arena.   There are more
PATIENTS in the background listening.   The
entire group composes a tableau.   The bath, in
which MARAT stands, is wheeled in through the
door at the back right.

CHORUS in sections:
A drawn-out cat-call.
A long monotonous whistle.
A muffled trampling of feet.

> (MARAT is pushed in his bath to the center
> of the arena. He stands straight and looks
> towards the HERALD.)

HERALD

Marat is still in his bathtub confined
but politicians crowd into his mind
He speaks to them his last polemic fight
to say who should be tribune. It is almost night.
> (He gives the orchestra a sign with his
> staff. A flourish. The people in the tab-
> leau spring to life, stamp their feet,
> whistle and shout.)

KOKOL

Down with Marat

CUCURUCU

Don't let him speak

ROSSIGNOL

Listen to him he's got the right to speak

POLPOCH

Long live Marat

KOKOL

Long live Robespierre

CUCURUCU

Long live Danton

MARAT

> (Addressing the audience. During his entire
> speech he never turns to those present on
> the stage. It is obvious that his speech is
> imaginary.)

Fellow citizens
members of the National Assembly
our country is in danger

From every corner of Europe armies invade us
led by profiteers
who want to strangle us
and already quarrel over the spoils
And what are we doing
        (apathetic noises)
Our minister of war
whose integrity you never doubted
has sold the corn meant for our armies
for his own profit to foreign powers
and now it feeds the troops
who are invading us
        (Cries and whistles)

KOKOL

Lies

CUCURUCU

Throw him out

MARAT

The chief of our army Dumouriez

ROSSIGNOL

Bravo

POLPOCH

Long live Dumouriez

MARAT

against whom I've warned you continually
and whom you recently hailed as a hero
has gone over to the enemy

KOKOL

Shame

ROSSIGNOL

Bravo

CUCURUCU

Liar
> (Shuffling of feet.)

MARAT

Most of the generals
who wear our uniform
are sympathetic with the emigrés
and when the emigrés return
our generals will be out to welcome them

KOKOL

Execute them

CUCURUCU

Down with Marat

ROSSIGNOL

Bravo

POLPOCH

Long live Marat

MARAT

Our trusted minister of finance
the celebrated Monsieur Cambon
is issuing fake banknotes thus increasing infla-
    tion
and diverting a fortune into his own pocket
> (Whistles and stamping.)

ROSSIGNOL

Long live free enterprise

MARAT

And I am told
that Perregeaux our most intelligent banker
is in league with the English
and in his armoured vaults
is organising a centre of espionage against us

COULMIER

(Jumping up to protest.)
That's enough
We're living in eighteen hundred and eight
and the names which were dragged through
    the gutter then
have been deservedly rehabilitated
by the command of the Emperor

ROSSIGNOL

Go on

KOKOL

Shut up Marat

CUCURUCU

Shut his mouth

POLPOCH

Long live Marat

MARAT

(Interrupting.)
The people can't pay the inflated price of bread
Our soldiers march in rags
The counter-revolution has started a new civil
    war
and what are we doing
The farms we confiscated from the churches
    have so far produced nothing

to feed the dispossessed
and years have passed since I proposed these
    farms
should be divided into allotments
and given farm implements and seed
And why have we seen no communal workshops
which were to be started in the old monasteries
    and country houses
Those who have jobs
must sweat for agents stockbrokers and specu-
    lators
      (Wild cries.)
Fellow citizens
did we fight for the freedom of those
who now exploit us again

KOKOL

Sit down

ROSSIGNOL

Hear hear

CUCURUCU

Sit down

POLPOCH

Hear hear

MARAT

Our country is in danger
We talk about France
but who is France for
We talk about freedom
but who's this freedom for
Members of the National Assembly
you will never shake off the past

you'll never understand
the great upheaval in which you find yourselves

  (Whistles and cries of Boo.)

Why aren't there thousands of public seats
in this assembly
so anyone who wants
can hear what's being discussed

DUPERRET
What is he trying to do
He's trying to rouse the people again
Look who sits on the public benches
Knitting-women concierges and washerwomen
with no one to employ them any more
And who has he got on his side
Pickpockets layabouts parasites
who loiter in the boulevards
  (Indignation among the onlookers.)
and hang around the cafés

CUCURUCU
Wish we could

DUPERRET
Released prisoners
escaped lunatics
  (Tumult and whistling.)
Does he want to rule our country
with these

MARAT
You are liars
You hate the people
  (Cries of indignation.)

ROSSIGNOL

Well done Marat

POLPOCH

That's true

MARAT

You'll never stop talking of the people
as a rough and formless mass
Why
Because you live apart from them
You let yourselves be dragged into the Revolution
knowing nothing about its principles
Has not our respected Danton himself announced
that instead of banning riches
we should try
to make poverty respectable
And Robespierre
who turns white when the word force is used
doesn't he sit at high-class tables
making cultural conversation
by candlelight

(Tongue clicking.)

KOKOL

Shame

CUCURUCU

Down with Robespierre

POLPOCH

Long live Marat

ROSSIGNOL

Down with Danton

MARAT

And you still long to ape them
those powdered chimpanzees
Necker Lafayette Talleyrand

COULMIER

(Interrupting.)
That's enough
If you use any more of these passages
we agreed to cut
I will stop your play

MARAT

(Breaking in.)
and all the rest of them
What we need now is a true deputy of the people
one who's incorruptible
one we can trust
Things are breaking down things are chaotic
that is good
that's the first step
Now we must take the next step
and choose a man
who will rule for you

ROSSIGNOL

Marat for dictator

POLPOCH

Marat in his bathtub

KOKOL

Send him down the sewers

CUCURUCU

Dictator of the rats

MARAT

Dictator The word must be abolished
I hate anything to do with masters and slaves
I am talking about a leader
who in this hour of crisis
> (His words are drowned in the mighty
> tumult.)

DUPERRET

He's trying to incite them
to new murders

MARAT

We do not murder
we kill in self-defence
We are fighting
for our lives

DUPERRET

Oh if only we could have constructive thought
instead of agitation
If only beauty and concord could once more
    replace
hysteria and fanaticism
> (The FOUR SINGERS throw themselves on
> DUPERRET and stop his mouth.)

ROUX

> (Jumping up in the background.)
Look what's happening
Join together
Cast down your enemies
disarm them
For if they win
they will spare
not one of you

and all that you have won so far
will be lost
> (Enthusiastic calls, whistles and tram-
> pling.)

CALLS
> (In spoken chorus, simultaneously.)

Marat Marat Marat Marat
Boo
A laurel wreath for Marat
Down with Marat
A victory parade for Marat
Down with him
Long live the streets
Long live the lamp-posts
Long live the bakers' shops
Long live freedom
> (Disorder and screams. The PATIENTS
> tumble forward. Marat's bath is pushed
> on to the platform right.)

KOKOL and POLPOCH
> (Dancing.)

Hit at the rich until they crash
Throw down their god and divide their cash

CUCURUCU and
ROSSIGNOL
> (Dancing.)

We wouldn't mind a tasty meal
of paté de foie and filleted eel

CHORUS
Marat Marat Marat Marat Marat
> (SADE raises his hands. They all freeze.
> Roll of drums and beginning of music.)

28.   POOR MARAT IN YOUR BATHTUB SEAT

>(MARAT sinks back into his bath.   Exhausted,
>he leans forward on the board. The specta-
>tors' benches are pushed back, the SISTERS
>and NURSES force back the PATIENTS.   In
>front of the arena the FOUR SINGERS dance
>a slow Carmagnole.)

[Poor Marat In Your Bathtub Seat]

FOUR SINGERS
(Accompanied, singing and dancing.)
Poor Marat in your bathtub seat
your life on this planet is near complete
Closer and closer to you death creeps
though there on her bench Charlotte Corday sleeps

Poor Marat if she slept too late
while dreaming of fairy-tale heads of state
maybe your sickness would disappear
Charlotte Corday would not find you here

Poor Marat stay wide awake
and be on your guard for the people's sake
Stare through the failing evening light
for this is the evening before the night

>(Drums.   In the background order has been
>restored after a fashion.   The PATIENTS
>should be standing upright, their hands
>crossed above their heads. SISTERS are
>standing before them, folding their hands
>and praying.   The murmur of prayers can be
>heard.   The FOUR SINGERS dance on a while
>and then stretch themselves out on the arena
>before Marat's bath.)

MARAT
(With fear in his voice.)
What is that knocking Simonne
(Tyrannic again.)
Simonne
more cold water
(SIMMONE sits huddled up at the edge of
the platform and doesn't react.)
Simonne
Where is Bas

SADE
Give up Marat
You said yourself
nothing can be achieved by scribbling
Long ago I abandoned my masterpiece
a roll of paper thirt; .ards long
which I filled completely with minute handwriting
in my dungeon years ago
It vanished when the Bastille fell
it vanished as everything written
everything thought and planned
will disappear
(MARAT lies with his face on the board
and covers his ears with his hands.)

SADE
(Continues.)
Marat
Look at me
Marat can you call this living
in your bath
in your mortification
(By order of the SISTERS the PATIENTS
change their position and stretch up their
hands.)

MARAT
(Raising himself up.)
I had time for nothing but work
Day and night were not enough for me
When I investigated a wrong it grew branches
and every branch grew twigs
Wherever I turned
I found corruption
(A PATIENT falls over in the ranks. A
NURSE carries him off.)
When I wrote
I always wrote with action in mind
kept sight of the fact
that writing was just a preparation
When I wrote
I always wrote in a fever
hearing the roar of action
When I was preparing
my book on the chains of slavery
I sat for three months
twenty-one hours a day
collecting material dreaming of material
paper piling high parchment crackling
until I sank into the swamps of overwork
That manuscript was suppressed
They were always ready
to pick up my statements
to slander them maim them
After each pamphlet was published
I had to go into hiding
They came with cannons
A thousand men of the National Guard
surrounded my house
And even today
I still wait for the knocking at the door
wait
for the bayonet to point at my breast

Simonne
Simonne
Fetch Bas
so that I can dictate my call
my fourteenth of July call

                        SADE
Why all these calls to the nation
It's too late Marat
forget your call
it contains only lies
What do you still want from the revolution
Where is it going
Look at these lost revolutionaries
        (Pointing to the FOUR SINGERS who lie
        stretched out on the floor, scratching
        themselves, yawning and trying to get the
        last drop out of the empty bottle.)
What will you order them to do
Where will you lead them
        (In the background the PATIENTS, on the
        Sisters' command, must stand on one leg.)
Once you attacked the authorities who turned
the law into instruments of oppression
Do you want someone to rule you
to control the words you write
and tell you
what work you must do
and repeat to you the new laws
over and over
until you can recite them in your sleep

        (The PATIENTS in the background walk in
        a circle while the SISTERS pray. The FOUR
        SINGERS begin to hum unconcernedly, lying
        at first on the floor with legs waving in
        the air. Then ROSSIGNOL and

CUCURUCU get up and dance to the
hummed melody.)

MARAT
(Falling across the board again.)
Why is everything so confused now
Everything I wrote or spoke
was considered and true
each argument was sound
And now
doubt
Why does everything sound false
(Singing and dancing.)

THE FOUR SINGERS
Poor old Marat you lie prostrate
while others are gambling with France's fate
Your words have turned into a flood
which covers all France with her people's blood
(Music ends. The FOUR SINGERS dance
back to the centre of the stage. The
PATIENTS are led to their platform. The
SISTERS try to wake CORDAY. Loud
knocking three times.)

29. PREPARATIONS FOR THE THIRD VISIT

HERALD
Corday
wake up
(Pause. The name CORDAY is whispered in
the background. The whispering swells up
and spreads over the whole stage. The SIS-
TERS shake CORDAY, DUPERRET calls
her name. SIMONNE stands awkwardly by
the bath a. .d gazes across at CORDAY.)

CHORUS

Corday
Corday
Corday

HERALD
(Signals to the orchestra with his staff.)
Corday you have an appointment to keep
and there is no more time for sleep
Charlotte Corday awake and stand
Take the dagger in your hand
> (Pause. The SISTERS raise CORDAY to her
> feet. CORDAY stands with lowered head
> and wobbly legs. The SISTERS support her
> and lead her slowly forward. Her legs drag
> along the floor. DUPERRET walks behind
> her with his hands around her hips.)

HERALD
Come on Charlotte do your deed
soon you'll get all the sleep you need
> (CORDAY is pushed into the arena. The
> two SISTERS stand at her side holding her
> firmly. DUPERRET, standing behind her,
> supports her back. Music ends.)

CORDAY
(Her eyes still closed, speaking softly,
nervously.)
Now I know what it is like
when the head is cut off the body
Oh this moment
hands tied behind the back
feet bound together
neck bared
hair cut off
knees on the boards

the head already laid
in the metal slot
looking down into the dripping basket
The sound of the blade rising
and from its slanting edge
the blood still drops
and then the downward slide
to split us in two
     (Pause.)
They say
that the head
held high in the executioner's hand
still lives
that the eyes still see
that the tongue still writhes
and down below the arms and legs still shudder

DUPERRET
     (Accompanied by lute.   He is still holding
     his hand on her hip.)
Charlotte awaken from your nightmare
Wake up Charlotte and look at the trees
look at the rose-coloured evening sky
in which your lovely bosom heaves
     (Pause.   He lifts his hand and strokes her
     on the bosom.   He notices the dagger un-
     der the cloth.)
Forget your worries abandon each care
and breathe in the warmth of the summer-
    time air
What are you hiding
A dagger
throw it away
     (The music ends.)

CORDAY
     (Pushes his hand away.)

We should all carry weapons nowadays
in self-defence

DUPERRET
(Beseechingly.)
No one will attack you Charlotte
Charlotte throw the dagger away
go away
go back to Caen

CORDAY
(Drawing herself up and pushing the
Sisters' hands away.)
In my room in Caen
on the table under the open window
lies open The Book of Judith
Dressed in her legendary beauty
she entered the tent of the enemy
and with a single blow
slew him

DUPERRET
Charlotte
what are you planning

CORDAY
(Forlorn again.)
Look at this city
Its prisons are crowded
with our friends
I was among them just now
in my sleep
They all stand huddled together there
and hear through the windows
the guards talking about executions
Now they talk of people as gardeners talk of
    leaves for burning

Their names are crossed off the top of a list
and as the list grows shorter
more names are added at the bottom
I stood with them
and we waited
for our own names to be called

DUPERRET

Charlotte
let us leave together
this very evening

CORDAY
(As if she has not heard him.)
What kind of town is this
What sort of streets are these
Who invented this
who profits by it
I saw peddlers
at every corner
they're selling little guillotines
with tiny sharp blades
and dolls filled with red liquid
which spurts from the neck
when the sentence is carried out
What kind of children are these
who can play
with this toy so efficiently
and who is judging
who is judging
(PATIENTS move to a group at centre.
CORDAY raises her hand to knock.)

30. CORDAY'S THIRD AND LAST VISIT

(The HERALD knocks three times on the
floor with his staff while CORDAY carries
out the knocking movement with her hand.
MARAT starts up and looks in Corday's
direction. SIMONNE places herself protec-
tively in front of the bath.)

DUPERRET
What do you want at this door
Do you know who lives here

CORDAY
The man
for whose sake I have come here

DUPERRET
What do you want from him
Turn back Charlotte
(Goes on his knees before her.)

CORDAY
I have a task
which I must carry out
Go
(Pushes him with her foot.)
leave me alone
(DUPERRET embraces her legs. She kicks
out at him several times. DUPERRET
moves back on his knees.)

HERALD
Now for the third time you observe
the girl whose job it is to serve
(Points to CORDAY.)
as Charlotte Corday stands once more

waiting outside Marat's door
Duperret you see before her languish
        (Points to DUPERRET.)
prostrated by their parting's anguish
        (Raising a forefinger.)
For what has happened cannot be undone
although that might be wished by everyone
        (Pointing to CORDAY.)
We tried restraining her with peaceful sleep
and with the claims of a passion still more deep
Simonne as well as best she could she tried
        (Pointing to SIMONNE.)
but this girl here
        (Points to CORDAY.)
would not be turned aside
That man is now forgotten and we can
        (Points to DUPERRET, who moves back-
        wards on his knees from the dais.)
Do nothing more Corday is focussed on this man
        (Points to MARAT.)

MARAT
No
        (Raising himself high.)
I am right
and I will say it once more
Simonne
where is Bas
It is urgent
my call
        (SIMONNE moves aside, stops still and
        stares bewitched at CORDAY.)

SADE
        (Approaches the bath.)
Marat
what are all your pamphlets and speeches

compared with her
she stands there and will come to you
to kiss you and embrace you
Marat
an untouched virgin stands before you and offers
     herself to you
See how she smiles

> (CORDAY stands erect and smiling, throw-
> ing her hair aside. She has her hand on
> the neckcloth in the place where the dagger
> is hidden.)

how her teeth shine
how she shakes her auburn hair aside
Marat
forget the rest
there's nothing else
beyond the body
Look
she stands there
her breast naked under the thin cloth
and perhaps she carries a knife
to intensify the love-play

> (CORDAY moves a step closer to the bath,
> swaying lightly. SIMONNE stands frozen,
> mechanically wringing the cloth in her
> hands.)

the body/sex is all there is

MARAT

Simonne Simonne
who was knocking at the door

SADE

A maiden
from the rural desert of a convent
Imagine
those pure girls lying on hard floors
in rough shifts

and the heated air from the fields
forcing its way to them through the barred windows
Imagine
them lying there
with moist thighs and breasts
dreaming of those
who control life in the outside world
> (The FOUR SINGERS come forward and
> begin a copulation mime.   ROSSIGNOL
> mounts the strongest of her companions
> and performs acrobatics with them.)

SADE
> (To musical accompaniment.)
And then she was tired of her isolation
and stirred up by the new age
and gathered up in the great tide
and wanted to be part of the Revolution
And what's the point of a revolution
without general copulation

[Copulation Round]

CHORUS
And what's the point of a revolution
without general
copulation copulation copulation
> (Continues as a round.   Mime ends.)

SADE
Marat
as I sat there in the Bastille
for thirteen long years
I learned
that this is a world of bodies
each body pulsing with a terrible power
each body alone and racked with its own unrest
In that loneliness

marooned in a stone sea
I heard lips whispering continually
and felt all the time
in the palms of my hands and in my skin
touching and stroking
Shut behind thirteen bolted doors
my feet fettered
I dreamed only
of the orifices of the body
put there
so one may hook and twine oneself in them
          (A PATIENT comes forward on tip-toe and
          stops behind the arena, listening tensely.
          Other PATIENTS follow.)
Continually I dreamed of this confrontation
and it was a dream of the most savage jealous
and cruellest imagining
Marat
these cells of the inner self
are worse than the deepest stone dungeon
and as long as they are locked
all your revolution remains
only a prison mutiny
to be put down
by corrupted fellow-prisoners

CHORUS
          (Repeating with musical accompaniment.)
And what's the point of a revolution
without general copulation
          (Music ends.)

CORDAY
          (To SIMONNE. Lute accompaniment.)
Have you given my letter to Marat
Let me in it is vital
I must tell him what's happening in Caen
where they are gathering to destroy him

MARAT

Who's at the door

SIMONNE

The girl from Caen

MARAT

Let her come in
> (SIMONNE stands aside, shaking her head
> vigorously. She squats down at the edge
> of the dais behind the bath and hides her
> head in her hands. CORDAY moves toward
> the bath, swaying and smiling. Her hand
> still rests on her neckcloth. SADE leaves
> the arena and goes to his dais, where he
> remains, standing, watching tensely.)

CORDAY

> (Softly.)

Marat
I will tell you the names of my heroes
but I am not betraying them
for I am speaking to a dead man

MARAT

> (Raising himself up.)

Speak more clearly
I can't understand you
Come closer

CORDAY

> (Coming closer to the bath with a fixed
> smile, her body slowly swaying. She pushes
> a hand under her neckcloth.)

I name you names
Marat
the names of those

who have gathered at Caen
          (falling into a sing-song)
I name Barbaroux
and Buzot
and Pétion
and Louvet
          (As she speaks the names her face is dis-
          torted increasingly by an expression of
          hate and lust.)
and Brissot
and Vergniaud
and Guadet
and Gensonné

MARAT

Who are you
Come closer
          (MARAT raises himself up high. The cloth
          falls from his shoulders. CORDAY moves
          closer to him, swaying. Her left hand is
          stretched out as if to caress. In the right
          hand she holds the dagger under the neck-
          cloth.)

CORDAY
          (Humming words which sound like caresses.)
I am coming Marat
You cannot see me Marat
because you are dead

MARAT
          (Crying out, raising himself up high, half-
          naked.)
Bas
Take this down
Saturday the thirteenth of July seventeen hundred
          and ninety three

A call to the people of France
> (CORDAY stands immediately before MA-
> RAT. She moves her left hand close to his
> skin over his chest, his shoulders, his neck.
> MARAT sits arched over the back of the
> bath, a pen still in his hand. CORDAY pulls
> the dagger from her neckcloth. She holds
> it with both hands and raises her arms high
> to strike. The HERALD blows shrilly on his
> whistle. All players remain unmoving in
> their positions. CORDAY sinks back into
> herself. MARAT sits quietly, leaning
> forward.)

31. INTERRUPTUS

HERALD

Now it's a part of Sade's dramatic plan
to interrupt the climax so this man
Marat can hear and gasp with his last breath
at how the world will go after his death
With a musical history we'll bring him up to date
From seventeen-ninety-three to eighteen-eight
> (Music starts with very quick military
> march. The FOUR SINGERS sing and
> perform grotesquely in time to the music.
> The HERALD displays banners showing the
> date of the events as they are described.)

FOUR SINGERS

Now your enemies fall
We're beheading them all (1793)
Duperret
and Corday
executed in the same old way
Robespierre has to get on (1794)
he gets rid of Danton

That was spring
comes July
and old Robespierre has to die
Three rebellions a year (1795)
but we're still of good cheer
Malcontents
all have been
taught their lesson by the guillotine
There's a shortage of   wheat (1796)
We're too happy to eat
Austria
cracks and then
she surrenders to our men

[Fifteen Glorious Years *]*

Fifteen glorious years
Fifteen glorious years
Years of peace
years of war
each year greater
than the year before
Marat
we're marching on

What brave soldiers we've got (1797)
Now the traitors are shot
Generals
boldly take
power in Paris
for the people's sake
Egypt's beaten down flat (1798)
Bonaparte did that
Cheer him as
they retreat
even though we lose our fleet
Bonaparte comes back (1799)

gives our rulers the sack
He's the man (1800)
brave and true
Bonaparte would die for you
Europe's free of her chains (1801)
Only England remains
but we want (1802)
wars to cease
so there's fourteen months of peace

(PATIENTS join in, marching on the spot.)
Fifteen glorious years
Fifteen glorious years
Years of peace
years of war
each year greater
than the year before
Marat
we're marching on

England must be insane (1803)
wants to fight us again
so we march
off to war
Bonaparte is our Emperor (1804)
Nelson bothers our fleet
but he's shot off his feet
We're on top
yes we are
and we spit on Trafalgar
Now the Prussians retreat (1806)
Russia faces defeat (1807)
All the world
bends its knee
to Napoleon
and his family
Fight on land and on sea (1808)

Act II

All men want to be free
If they don't
never mind
we'll abolish all mankind

Fifteen glorious years
Fifteen glorious years
Years of peace
years of war
each year greater
than the one before
Marat
we're marching on
behind Napoleon

32. THE MURDER

(The entire cast have resumed their positions
exactly as before the song. CORDAY clasps
the knife with both hands above her head. Very
slowly she lowers it toward MARAT. SADE
follows her movements precisely, bending
from the waist. She kills MARAT. PATIENTS
let out one single scream. CORDAY crumples
on the stage. SADE stands contemplating the
scene. MARAT hangs as in David's classical
picture, with his right hand over the edge of
the bath. In his right hand he still holds his
pen, in his left his papers.)

HERALD

Tell us Monsieur de Sade for our instruction
just what you have achieved with your production.
Who won? Who lost? We'd like to know
the meaning of your bath-house show

SADE

Our play's chief aim has been--to take to bits
great propositions and their opposites,

see how they work, then let them fight it out.
The point? Some light on our eternal doubt.
I have twisted and turned them every way
and find no ending to our play.
Marat and I both advocated force
but in debate each took a different course.
Each wanted changes, but his views and mine
on using power never can combine.
On the one side he who thinks our lives
can be improved with axes and knives.
Or--the one who'd submerge in his imagination
seeking a personal annihilation.
So for me the last word cannot ever be spoken.
I am left with a question that's always open.

33. EPILOGUE

> (The ORCHESTRA starts to play soft cere-
> monious music. The SISTERS come forward
> and take charge of CORDAY. MARAT steps
> out of his bath. COULMIER comes forward.)

COULMIER
Enlightened ladies pious gentlemen
let's close the history book and then
return to eighteen-eight the present day
of which though not unclouded we may say
it promises that mankind soon will cease
to fear the storms of war the squalls of peace
> (The music turns more and more into a
> monotonous march. The PATIENTS in the
> background mark time. Their unrest in-
> creases.)
For today we live in far different times
We have no oppressors no violent crimes
and although we're at war anyone can see
it can only end in victory

[Finale]

FOUR SINGERS

And if most have a little and few have a lot
you can see how much nearer our goal we have got
We can say what we like without favour or fear
and what we can't say we can breathe in your ear

ROUX

(Through the singing.)
When will you learn to see
When will you learn to take sides
When will you show them.

FOUR SINGERS

And though we're locked up we're no longer
    enslaved
and the honour of France is eternally saved
The useless debate the political brawl
are over there's one man to speak for us all
For he helps us in sickness and destitution
he's the leader who ended the Revolution
and everyone knows why we're cheering for
Napoleon our mighty Emperor

> (During the song COULMIER and his family
> have congratulated SADE and chatted with him.
> SADE presents various members of the cast.
> At this point the music grows louder. The
> column of PATIENTS begins to march forward.
> SISTERS and NURSES try to restrain it. Sev-
> eral times the column advances four paces
> and takes three paces back. The music and
> marching rhythm grow in power. COULMIER
> moves anxiously to the side gesticulating.)

ALL

Led by him our soldiers go
over deserts and through the snow
A victory here and a victory there
Invincible glorious always victorious

for the good of all people everywhere
>   (The column advances still further, stamping
>   some paces forward and some back. The
>   HERALD begins to throw buckets etc. around.
>   NURSES try to restrain him. Coulmier's
>   family flee, screaming and shouting.)

ALL
>   (In confused but rhythmic shouts in time to
>   the marching.)
Charenton Charenton
Napoleon Napoleon
Nation Nation
Revolution Revolution
Copulation Copulation
>   (The shouting grows. The column reaches
>   the front. The struggle between NURSES
>   and HERALD develops and catches the at-
>   tention of the others. Suddenly the whole
>   stage is fighting. SADE watches with a faint
>   smile, almost indulgent. The actors have
>   moved to the side. Music, shouting and
>   tramping increase to a tempest. A strong
>   wind blows in through the upper side windows.
>   The huge curtains billow far into the room.
>   The NURSES go among the patients wielding
>   their batons. ROUX springs forward and
>   places himself before the marchers, his back
>   to them, still with fettered arms.)

ROUX
When will you learn to see
When will you learn to take sides
>   (He tries to force them back, but is drawn
>   in and vanishes from sight in the still ad-
>   vancing ranks. The PATIENTS are fully at

the mercy of their mad marchlike dance. Many of them hop and spin in ecstasy. COULMIER incites the NURSES to extreme violence. PA-TIENTS are struck down. The HERALD is now in front of the orchestra, leaping about in time to the music. SADE stands upright on his chair, laughing triumphantly. In despera-tion COULMIER gives the signal to close the curtain.)

CURTAIN

NOTES ON CHARACTERS

AND COSTUMES

MARQUIS DE SADE: He is sixty-eight years old, extremely corpulent, with gray hair and smooth complexion. He moves heavily, breathes at times with difficulty, as if asthmatic. His clothing is of good quality, but worn. He is wearing white breeches with bows, a wide-sleeved white shirt with ornamental front and lace cuffs and white buckled shoes.

JEAN-PAUL MARAT: He is in his fiftieth year, and suffering from a skin disease. He is draped in a white cloth and has a white bandage round his temples.

SIMONNE EVRARD: Marat's mistress is of indeterminate age. The player of the role is wearing a hospital uniform, with an apron and a headcloth. Her posture is crooked, her movements odd and constrained. When she has nothing to do, she stands wringing a cloth in her hands. She seizes every opportunity to change Marat's bandage.

CHARLOTTE CORDAY: She is twenty-four years of age. Her clothing consists of a thin white blouse of Empire cut. The blouse does not conceal the bosom, but she wears a flimsy white cloth over it. Her long auburn hair hangs down on the right side of her neck. She wears pink leather boots with high heels, and when she is "on stage" a ribboned hat is tied on her. She is attended throughout by two Sisters, who support her, comb her hair and arrange her clothes. She moves like a somnambulist.

DUPERRET: Duperret is a Girondist Deputy. The player of the role wears, in addition to his hospital shirt, a short waistcoat and the smooth tight trousers of an "Incroyable." His clothing is also white, with some ornamentation. He is held in the mental home as an erotomaniac, and takes advantage of his role as Corday's lover at every suitable opportunity.

JACQUES ROUX: He is a former priest, a radical Socialist. He wears a white hospital shirt with an overall shaped like a monk's robe. The sleeves of his shirt are tied together in front of him over his hands, and he can move only in the limits of this straitjacket.

THE FOUR SINGERS: Kokol, Bass; Polpoch, Baritone; Cucurucu, Tenor; Rossignol, Soprano. They are part crowd types, part comedians. They have decked out their hospital uniforms with grotesque bits of costume and wear the cap of the Revolution. Rossignol, with her tricolour sash and sabre, represents the figure of Marianne. They have singing voices and perform in mime.

PATIENTS: The patients serve as extras, voices, mimes and chorus. According to need they appear either in their white hospital uniforms or in primitive costumes with strong colour contrasts. Any not required in the play devote themselves to physical exercises. Their presence must set the atmosphere behind the acting area. They make habitual movements, turn in circles, hop, mutter to themselves, wail, scream and so on.

HERALD: He wears a harlequin smock over his hospital shirt. His two-pointed cap is hung with bells and spangles. He is draped with numerous instruments with which he can make a noise as necessary. He holds in his hand a beribboned staff.

FIVE MUSICIANS: They are inmates of the mental home, clad in white. They play harmonium, lute, flute, trumpet and drums.

MALE NURSES: They wear light gray uniforms with long white aprons, which give them the appearance of butchers. They carry batons in the pockets of their aprons.

SISTERS: They also are dressed in light gray, with long white aprons, starched collars and large white bonnets. They carry rosaries. The Sisters are played by athletic-looking men.

COULMIER: The director of the mental home is elegant in light gray clothing, with coat and top hat. He wears pince-nez and carries a walking stick.   He likes to adopt a Napoleonic pose.

COULMIER'S WIFE and DAUGHTER: They form a composite pattern of colour from pale mauve to pearl gray, sprinkled with jewels and glittering silver.

PROPERTIES

GENERAL:

Bathtubs, showers, platforms, benches, massage tables, railing and curtains, dais for Marat's bath, dais for Sade's chair, two tribunals. Marat's bathtub should be equipped with wheels.

PERSONAL:

MARAT: Sheet, bandage, pen and inkwell, papers on board, map of France.
HERALD: Staff, rattle, Pan-flute, whistle, banners bearing dates from 1793 to 1808.
CORDAY: Neck cloth, dagger, letter.
KOKOL: Wreath of leaves, bucket.
COULMIER: Stick (cane).
SIMONNE: Jug.
FOUR SINGERS: Playing cards, dice, bottle.
TWO PATIENTS: Cloth cover (to represent horse), cart.
CUCURUCU: Cross made of broomsticks.
POLPOCH: Rope around neck.
ROSSIGNOL: Beads.
A PATIENT: Clerical collar.
NURSES: Straps (to fasten Roux), batons.
SADE: Whip.
SCHOOLMASTER: Cane.
LAVOISIER: Palm branch.